FAST TRACK
to
Romance

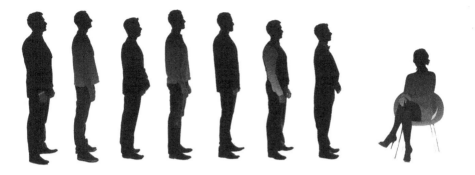

FAST TRACK

to

Romance

*An exclusive online dating
guide for the mature woman*

GAIL KARPUS

For information about this title or to order other books and/or electronic media, contact the publisher:

Gail Karpus
gailkarpus@yahoo.com

ISBNs:0999830600
978-0-9998306-0-4 Print
978-0-9998306-1-1 eBook

Printed in the United States of America

Cover and Interior design: 1106 Design

Dedication

*For my husband, Paul, whose insight, support, and love
made this book possible.*

*And, thanks to my good friend Sandy, who inspired me
to write this book and stayed along for the ride.*

Table of Contents

TWENTY-FIVE

——————

TWENTY-SIX

——————

CHAPTER ONE

It's Time for You to Find Romance

I've heard it said that you have to kiss a lot of frogs to find your prince . . . Well . . . Then my face should be covered with warts!

*t*he saying, "Love needs no map because it can find its way blindfolded" is a lovely quote—but really? Maybe with a cane and a good-looking guide dog by your side . . .

Hey, it's hard to find love at any point in life, but when you're an older woman, it gets a lot harder. But, like anything else worth getting, you have to work at it.

In today's world, online dating is the smart way, the most solid way to find romance. Men especially like dating online, and it is their choice for finding romance. Why? It's the easiest way for them to find a date or a mate without direct, face-to-face rejection. They have spent years chasing women, and with that comes rejection. It's a lot easier to get over rejection from a computer.

Many older women *don't* go online because they are afraid of the unknown. So many single ladies tell me, "I don't even know where to start!" They're fearful about making mistakes or meeting up with a "stranger"! Some feel their friends and relatives will think they are crazy or desperate to go online for a date. They tell them, "Don't you know there are crazy people out there?" Plus, if you're an older woman, whether single, divorced, or widowed, you are most likely used to the man asking you to go out on a date. It doesn't feel normal to you or your ego to go looking for someone—especially on a computer! I get that.

But, times have changed. It's the computer age, and people want immediate satisfaction today. But, it's also a time when the age limits have changed! Today, 80 is the "new 70," 70 is the "new 60," 60 is the "new 50," and so on. Happily, we live better and longer, and we are living in a time in which we have access to "age defying" products and cosmetic procedures to help keep us looking and feeling young!

I've heard many women say they believe they're too old, too round, too set in their ways. Afraid to consider online dating. Afraid to even consider another romance or marriage, even though they would really like to have "that someone" to share their life with. Of course, this attitude is not representative of all the single, mature women out there. After all, not all women are searching for someone new in their life. Some gals just opt for hanging out with girlfriends, drinking wine, and watching the Hallmark channel. Hey, non-stop, voracious reading with the remote in your hand can be pretty darn good! Some gals feel they are happy with the way their life is already going. Who needs a man? There are other ways to be fulfilled today—and let's be real: All you need is batteries. Why complicate things?

Yes, that may be true for some, but from what I've heard from the majority of single women and men is that they *do* want someone constant in their life. They want that "partner in crime," that one person they can count on in good times and in bad. "The bacon to their eggs!" A Lady and the Tramp sharing that plate of spaghetti, maybe a glass of wine, while listening to the crooning of Frank Sinatra or the sounds of a big band. And, who doesn't want or need that Nurse Nightingale who will watch over you during the night when you've got a cold or the flu?

Most people would like to have a happy life of their own and be independent of their children (if you have them) financially and socially. It's natural for someone to want their kids to know that mom is cared for and loved by someone—that they don't have to worry about a "place for mom," or whether she'll live in their converted garage or an unaffordable independent-living residence. No mother or father wants to burden their children with the task of finding them a suitable lifestyle and having to pay for it. Maybe your children are already striving to put your grandkids through college or trying to save money for their own retirement.

Possibly, you are alone as a result of losing a mate. Maybe you've never found one. Maybe it's not even money that concerns you. Maybe you just like male companionship. You still have a lot of living to do, and maybe you want the comfort of a gentleman to help you enjoy it. Someone you can lean on, feel safe with, and have fun with! A person worthy of what you have to offer.

Well, you *can* have that. I promise you: It's out there waiting for you! It's called *online dating*—no matter what your age is. It's a vehicle, ready and waiting for you as a way to have fun and meet new people—others who are also looking to have someone special in their life. But, you need to go out and get it! It won't just come to you. So, consider this handbook as your personal guide that will fast-track you to getting online as quickly and as easily as possible—and to become successful at it, all while having great fun!

Believe me, I know how hard it is to start this process. And, I certainly know how difficult it can be to say the right words in a profile or to put up the right pictures. When I first started online dating 11 years ago, I spent those years changing pictures and writing different types of profiles, trying to romantically market myself to the masses of men online—and there are masses of men online. And, yes, you *are* marketing yourself, just like you did in the old days, but in a different venue.

Let me tell you a little about me and why I know I can help you. You can date online while feeling positive about yourself and the people you'll meet.

I started online dating in 2005, when I arrived in Beverly Hills (BH), California after a divorce. I didn't know anyone except my children and their mates. I didn't have anyone to go out with or ways to meet people, and I didn't want to go out alone. Now, it's rough dating *anywhere* as an older woman, but in Southern California? Well, it is *really* challenging. Hey, it is home to some of the most beautiful people in the world and loaded with a lot more single women than men. New crops of hopeful lovelies wanting to get into the movies arrive here daily. Maybe they don't make it into the movies, but most of them stay anyway. All the while, they're aging, and, eventually, they become the "older crowd."

Now, remember: When I started online dating, it was 2005, and it was still strange to go to a bar alone without looking like you wanted to get—ahem—*some action.*

But certainly, I didn't want to sit home alone, all dressed up with no place to go! What to do? Well, my beautiful, smart daughter and I devised a plan to get around this. I went to a very high-end restaurant in BH, walked in, and sat at the bar. I didn't want to seem like I was an escort or something like that. But, I was dressed for the cocktail hour! So, to make it look like I wasn't supposed to be just by myself at the bar, my daughter would call me on my cell phone about five minutes after my arrival. I'd answer, still sitting at the bar, and speak so I could be heard by a few people around me, but I wasn't loud. The contrived conversation consisted of why she (supposedly, my girlfriend) couldn't meet me. She'd say that her babysitter didn't show up, or that she'd broken a front tooth—or just about anything we thought believable. After all, I didn't want it to sound canned. We would speak to each other like this was really "happening."

There are always men sitting at a bar around cocktail hour. I'd tell "my friend" how sorry I was that she couldn't meet me but that I totally understood her situation. I'd hang up and sigh slightly. That led to at least one guy (or more) coming and sitting down next to me. Even the bartender would commiserate with me and say, "Sorry, but I couldn't help overhear about your friend not being able to meet you." It was an icebreaker, and I didn't feel out of place. My daughter and I did "the call' a few times but not at the same restaurant or hotel bar. It got me out of the house, and it got results. I met a few nice guys that way. Yes, it was a little white lie. But, hey: As the saying goes, "A girl's gotta do what a girl's gotta do!"

But, I needed a better approach to find dates. *Voila!* Online dating was in its early stages. My daughter suggested that I try it. That allowed her not to have to act as my "call center," too.

The first online dating site I got on was *JDate.com*. It is a site geared for Jewish men and women to meet people within their religion—but, it wasn't strict, by any means. I wasn't Jewish, but I had been married to a Jewish man for 20 years, and, while I hadn't converted, I knew the culture well. I was comfortable dating the men who were on there and they me. Then, I found *Match.com* and joined that site. Soon, online dating became my only source for meeting men and dating. It also helped me to meet gal friends! The guys I met would take me to their friends' parties. There were a group of single, well-off men in Hollywood Hills in those days. They would gather up girls for each other's parties. Fresh meat, I guess. They called themselves the "Wolf Pack," and, yes—they were!

After living in LA for a few years, I had a sales position as a BH Italian wine rep, and later a sales rep in BH for an Italian food company. Soon after, I found myself working for one of Beverly Hills' top matchmaking companies. It was, to say the least, interesting—and informative.

I gathered knowledge of the how, the why, and the where people went to date. I learned what made successful matches.

I was a matchmaker in the matchmaking business! It was an eye-opener! But the best knowledge I gathered came from my own online dating—and lots of it. I learned the hard knocks of online dating over many, many years. What I write here is validated through my many experiences. No, I have not polled 100 online daters for their experiences, because *I am the poll.* I have had more than 500 meets/dates in these years. And last year, I met "the one." After four months, I married the most fantastic, wittiest, most successful man (aka "doctor"—what your mother always said you should marry)—a caring, thoughtful, kind, funny guy who rocks my world every day! We're perfect for each other! We can't believe how lucky we were to have found each other, and it was from an online dating site.

No, I wasn't being super picky for 11 years. There were many relationships, mostly short, a few long. Along the way of these sometimes bumpy but mostly fun online dating years, I was fortunate to meet some really great guys! So, you've gotta believe that there is that needle in the online-dating haystack! You just have be "in it to win it," and you must be persistent in finding it!

In 2011, I started writing online profiles for friends who really wanted to go online to date but just could not figure out what to say and how to go about it. After a while, friends were referring friends who asked me to please write their profiles. Seeing this need, I started a business called Heart Profile Service. I had some great success stories. I not only wrote their profiles, but I also had professional photos taken of them and helped them navigate through the online process. I even told them what to look for in other people's profiles! I felt good that I was able to help people find love in their golden years. Unfortunately, at the time, there was no way to market this type of business, because the dating sites wouldn't let me advertise my business on their sites. It made sense, because within a year or so of my start-up business, they were profiting themselves by writing profiles.

I am happy to say that there were success stories for these Baby Boomers. A 74-year-old Southern California man found his love in Utah after his wife had left him some years before. He was lonely and ready for love, and he found it online with my help. An 80-year-old woman who'd moved here from Dakota wanted to go online because she wanted companionship. She wasn't very familiar with the computer her daughter had bought her. I worked many hours, sitting side by side with her at the computer, going over profiles.

When I helped people get online, I always did a 2- to 3-hour interview with them. I wanted to get to know what type of person they were looking for. Most people have a list of what they want. I advise anyone who has a long list to take the top three important things that you can't live without in a mate and put those other traits on the side. Anyway, this adorable little 80-year-old widow said to me, "Be sure to put in my profile that I want to have sex!" LOL! Good for her! I told her I would put that in her profile but in a gentler way, using the words, "I still enjoy the 'intimacy' of a being with a gentleman. I still have a lot of passion to give." And guess what? She did find a like-minded gentle-man within a few weeks! It wasn't just about the sex. They became inseparable companions. But the implication sure was noticed by a man.

I have written profiles for women and men in their sixties who were newly divorced and skeptical about going online to find love. There is someone for everyone, and it is never too late to find romance. But, again, you won't find it if you don't look for it. You've gotta to be in the game to win it.

These are just a couple of the stories of people who, although they were already grandparents, decided that they didn't want to go through the rest of their life by themselves. How did they meet someone right away? They went online with good advice from me, along with current, professional pictures to immediately make that first, good impression on their choice of sites. They used pictures that showed them doing the things they loved to do—like gardening, cooking, dancing, hiking. You know what I mean—hobbies or passions that showed their personality.

The tips and messages in this book are meant to help you to find what you're looking for faster and with fewer road signs to slow down your journey. Like I said previously, there are many lonely people I meet who tell me that they just don't know if it's for them or that they have no idea how to even get started.

They tell me, "I'm afraid because of the horror stories I've heard from others. I'm too old to be looking for a new life. I don't think I can compete with the other women out there." They have so many concerns about saying the wrong thing or not being able to write about themselves. Its understandable. It can be scary to figure out what to say and how to say it when you get an online dater's email. Yow! *This guy wants to meet me!*

As I said before, today's online dating is the number-one most effective way to meet someone or to find a mate, especially if you are older than 50. You may not be attending the functions you did in your younger years that allowed you the opportunity to meet other people. As we age, we have less energy, retire earlier at night, and don't bar-hop like we used to—or not at all. We feel and see the changes within ourselves. Aging is just not fun—but it does happen to everyone. Ah, yes: We can fight the aging war, but there will be a time when the battle becomes futile, and that's when we say, "OK, we'll just age gracefully—maybe."

What You Should Know

Online dating is *fun* and *should* be fun for you if you have the right tools to approach it. As I said before, my goal is to fast-track you! I plan to arm you quickly and realistically with what you need to jump into the world of computer dating—to start or improve your dating online. You will become confident and not drown in the sea of unknowns. I want you to be successful in your pursuit!

Please don't listen to the people who say they tried online dating and it was terrible. They probably weren't using good techniques, didn't stick with it, or didn't work on it daily. Remember, their experience does not have to be your experience. You will find someone if you do the homework, follow the guidelines you find here, and have the persistence to search for the one you're looking for.

But, make no mistake: It takes time, thought, and tenacity. You'll need to keep your humor card out, because there will be times you'll need it. One other thing: You won't be bored.

The Different Types of Men You'll Meet

*i*t is safe to say you will be surprised by many of your meets. That is half the fun. Some will show up looking like bums—shorts, sandals, tee shirt, unshaven, a beard so full, he'll look like Grizzly Adams. I often wonder if the homeless guy I see looking for handouts on the corner could be my date, with a laptop. That cracks me up!

Some will show up like a photo from *Esquire* or *Gentleman's Quarterly* magazine: Dress pants, fine shirt, beautiful jacket, shined shoes. This one is my favorite, by the way.

Some will show up with tattoos everywhere or pick you up in one of those unbelievably large trucks. You're wearing 5" heels and trying to maneuver getting into his truck without your dress flying up to your face. They will show up with their very large dog, or an extreme amount of nose or ear hair, maybe a braid, even a motorcycle with a helmet for you (there goes your hair). The list is endless but interesting.

There will be some guys who, once you think about them, you will just end up shaking your head in wonder. Like this really nice guy I'll call "Hal."

I had a date with a Hal about three days after our first meet at a coffee shop. The date was to go to a dance club located about a mile from my apartment in West Los Angeles. The music didn't start till 10:00 PM, so we decided he should pick me up at 9:30 in the evening. He showed up to get me in one of his beautiful classic cars. We go to get in the car, and he walks to his side of the car, not mine. Now, I'm sorry: A gentleman opens a lady's door, especially on a first date! So, I just stood at my side of the car as he got into his. He looked up at me with a "What's up?" look. Hello! Did I verbally have to tell this guy to open my door and help me in the car? Well, he got out of the car and walked around, opened my door, with a shrug, and I got in. We had great conversation as we drove to the dance club.

He parks the car on the street near the club, opens my door, helps me out, and we go into the club and have drinks and dance for a couple of hours. We come out, and, again, he opens the door on my side of the car and helps me in. He goes around to the driver's side and gets in the car, flicks the key, starts the engine—nothing. The car does not start. No matter how many times he tries to start it, it's a no-go. He lifts the hood, checks everything, sees nothing wrong. Now his business is collecting and trading classic cars, so he knows exactly what to do mechanically with these classic cars. He did everything he could think of to get it going. He was perplexed, shaking his head, muttering to himself. He looks at me and says, with all seriousness, "I've never had a problem with this car. I think it's because I opened the door for you—I've never opened that door myself. Everyone else just gets in!" Seriously, I thought he was kidding—and maybe he was, just a tiny bit—but I think he really thought that was the reason the car would not start. Well, I couldn't help it. I started laughing so hard I had to get out of the car. It was a warm evening, so I sat chuckling on the curb while we waited for a tow truck to come get us. That took an hour, and, mind you, even though I'm sitting on the curb at midnight, I was really patient about the wait. The truck finally arrives; the driver tries to jump the car to get it to start—nothing. Lots of head shaking going on, and the end result is the car has to be towed away. We get in the cab of the tow truck with the driver, and we all go to the service station, unhook the car, and leave it. Now, it's 1:30 in the morning. Hal lives about twenty minutes away, and he was to go back to the service station to see the mechanic that same morning at 7 AM—in about only five hours. He was going to get himself a hotel room, but I told him he could stay in my living room. The station was only two miles away from where I lived, and I felt really bad for this guy. So, I pumped up the blow-up bed, and he stayed the night in my living room. He was a perfect gentleman. Next morning, he walked to get the car. In about twenty minutes, he is back at my apartment with a Starbucks coffee for me. He thanked me for letting him stay over, but when he got to the station, the car started right up—no problem. He proceeds to tell me he thinks that, because he opened my door so many times, I jinxed the car, and he doesn't want me to ride in the car again! He was serious. Obviously, I have magic powers I don't know about! *C'est la vie!*

Getting back to the types of men you'll meet: If I had to give you the top 10 types of men you'll most likely meet, they would be these:

The Whiner:

No—this has nothing to do with drinking wine, although the more he has, the more he may whine. This is the guy who complains about his terrible dates. He will say online meets don't look like their picture, they look older than he thought they'd look, he doesn't want to date his mother, etc. Yet he is in his 60s and doesn't realize he looks like your father. He will tell you, "You are the best online meet yet!" He will end up whining about traffic, waiting in line at a restaurant, or his little blue pill isn't working, so it must have been made in Mexico!

The Casanova:

He immediately touches your arm, talks very close and sexy to you, while his eyes are saying, "I want to bed you." He will tell you how beautiful you are and how he can't control himself in wanting you so much because he is so "taken" with you. He's sorry, but gee, he just can't help it.

He will usually kiss you within 15 or 30 minutes of meeting you and innocently ask you, "Oh—was that too soon?" If you're OK with it and are looking for the same thing—go for it!

The Know-It-All:

He will contradict everything you say and give you lengthy explanations of why and how he knows all this information. If you disagree with him, he will just think you're stupid.

He is extremely impatient with you. He even knows what's wrong with your life—and what you're doing or not doing to make it right.

The Nurturer:

He will want to help you with your problems and will advise you on how you or he can help make your life easier and better. He will go out of his way to help you in any way he can. Don't disregard him. You could do a lot worse!

The Comedian:

He will start with cute jokes that never end. He will go and on and even tell the server the same joke or one that he thinks is just as funny. He thinks he is the cleverest guy ever. He is literally entertaining himself and trying to impress you at the same time. If you have the same sense of humor and can banter back and forth with him, he just might be for you—if you have a huge amount of patience. But, if you can't take it, he's not for you. You will end up wanting to choke him at dinner by your second date.

The Vomiter :

No, he doesn't literally throw up his food, but he can't wait to tell you everything about him or his life in the first 10 minutes. He will tell you mostly the bad stuff about himself, his life, relationships, etc. He feels if he gets all this out right away, he won't have to worry about you being disappointed with him in the future. He may be an insecure guy. But more than likely, he is a straight-up "tell it like it is" guy. Again, you could do worse—well, unless he tells you he's been in prison for running a drug cartel. Actually, I did have a date who admitted he had gone to jail for two years for major drug dealing. And then there was the one who went to jail for tax evasion. OK, so maybe these were not the most honorable of guys, but they we're straight up!

The Bore:

He will go on and on and on about anything and every-thing that you probably do not care about. It doesn't matter how much you try to change the subject or steer him in a different direction—he will just have another boring (but important to him) story to tell you and facts that you don't care to even know about, ever. He doesn't care what you have to say or share with him. At some point, he may not even realize you're there. He is just going on and on and on. Yes: Index finger to your temple, and pull the trigger, because you will be thinking, *Please make him stop! I'm outta here!*

The Interview Bully:

He will fire one question after another at you, about your background, your lovers, your car, your income, etc. He is actually interrogating you to see if you are worth his time or dinner investments for future dates. If he is a sci-fi fan, and you're not, you are gone. If he runs 20 miles a day, and you don't, you are gone. If you don't make enough money—uh, huh: Gone again. He has a set amount of rules in his head about what he wants from a woman. He fast tracks every woman he meets.

He is not what you'd call a sensitive guy. The only way to deal with him is to push back. Tell him you don't give that type of information on a first meet. If he says, "Why not—are you hiding something?" (with a smile on his face). Ask him to produce his retirement portfolio and bank-accounts balances. His face will go blank. He may not get it. You can tell him it's personal and that he is not yet on an NTK (Need to Know) basis. He may lighten up on his questioning then, or he'll pull back altogether and end the interview—lucky you!

The Rock Star:

This one is easy to find in Los Angeles, California, and probably every other major city. He is gorgeous. I mean, you can be beautiful, but when the two of you walk into a restaurant or some other public place together, all eyes will be on him. He will have his actor face on (even if he's not one), those smiley (LA-made) white teeth, and that dreamy smile he has perfected so well.

His has a flashy car and a flashy house, and he dresses like the publisher of GQ. He is "matured," with hair that has just the right amount of gray at the temples (LA hairdressers at their best). He doesn't look his age by 20 years (LA plastic surgeons at their best).

He works out three hours a day, and he looks it. He is busy—very busy—and he will make dates and break dates, depending on who or what comes along. He will smile and turn on the charm at other women even while he's with you, but it's hard to be mad at him because you get it! If you are with him, good for you, because you can be sure it's because you're so "hot"—no matter your age! He is a bad, bad, boy. He will make you feel so "special" just to be with him. He's exciting to be with, but you probably won't be with him long. Either way, a girl's gotta give herself a ride with this one. He's really good for the morale, but he's probably not relationship-worthy. You'll eat well, though!

The Nice Guy

This guy is caring and sensitive to your wants and needs. He is a gentleman who will go out of his way to help others, and he will willingly try to make you feel special. You know when you meet him that he is just a nice, easy-going guy. Should you both fall in love, you'd be a very lucky gal.

"Love is like a fire. Whether it is going to warm your hearth or burn your house down, you'll never know." But, we all need a match to find out. Want a light?

CHAPTER THREE

Photos...Photos...Photos...

*Y*ou can't start online dating without them. Don't even try. You'll need the best ones that you can get of yourself. It is a waste of time to start the online process without good ones. Go for the gold right away! A man is extremely visual in his conception of what "rings his bell." Men surf the online dating sites. So, when they are surfing through a sea of photos on a site, your photo needs to make him *stop*, as in, "Whoa, boy!! Stop right there! Hmmm. I wonder what she's all about?" You want him to read your profile page right away to keep that interest going.

Pictures are worth a thousand words. To a man, this magnifies to a million words. I strongly suggest—and I can't say this too strongly—that you get professional photos taken. It's worth the effort to do it right the first time.

These photos should show spirit, playfulness, and sexiness in small doses. They should tell a story about you immediately. Say you're sitting on top of a desk with a business suit and heels, your legs crossed. It lends the idea of professionalism, strength, and sexiness. Get the idea? I promise you: A photo like that will get surf attention from the online lookers! If you like cooking, a photo of you in an apron and a chef's hat—and little else—is an attention-getter! Gardening—whatever. Think about any hobby or something you like to do, and make it look fun and sexy.

Now you may say, "That's really putting a sexual connotation on this! " *Yes, it is! Know your market!* You are marketing to men who want to get excited to meet you. When they see your photo, they need to feel excited to want to get to know the person they see in that photo. Hey! They're not shopping for furniture here. The same goes for you! We are all online because we're looking for love, and the first thing to excite anyone is the photo!!

Along With That: A Few Rules

There should be no other people in your photo!

Don't use a picture from which you've cut out another person. Anyone can still see that it was a picture of you with someone else. You might have left in a hand showing or made it look like an obvious photoshop. No matter that you think it was the best picture ever taken of you. It's not only unprofessional but sloppy, too!

Don't show pictures of you with a best friend or other people.

Just a photo of you! You don't want to confuse the looker into wondering which is you and which one is your friend.

Show sexiness, not hooker-ness. Classy wins.

No grandma shots with babies, kids . . . zilch!!!

A dog is OK, but please don't be like the guy who had 15 photos of his dog up. Plus a few more with him and the dog! I had that kind of first meet. When I went to meet him, he brought his dog along. I wasn't surprised. After all, there were 15 pictures of him and the dog. Well, on the chance he'd bring the dog, (yes, of course, he brought the dog), I had put some dog biscuits in my pocket. The dog smelled them immediately and started nudging me ever so strongly, so I kept petting him. The guy said, "I've never seen this dog so friendly with any of my first-meet gals! That is a definite plus for you." This dog really ruled this guy! If the dog is that important to him, that adored dog will always come before you! I will say this just as a minor point, but this would be a red flag that there might be other issues with him.

- Some of the comments he made told me this guy was what I would term "a loser." He told me how he'd lived with a woman (didn't want to get married) for eighteen years, but he never loved her. He said she was good for finances. How shallow is this guy? After 20 minutes of that type of conversation, I knew I was not interested in this guy at all. I got up to leave. I said to him, "It was nice to meet you." (It wasn't, but you need some decorum, right?) At that point, he asked for a next date with me right away. Now that's something neither he nor you should do, because it's awkward. I said, "No. Sorry. You're really not my type." He said to me, "I really am interested in you. I usually don't spend money on a woman, but I'd spend money on you."

- Really???? I mean, he met me outside a Starbucks and didn't even offer to buy me a cup of coffee. This guy wasn't poor. He told me he was an architect, made a great living, blah blah, blah. I bet he bought his dog $50 bags of dog food, but I also bet he wouldn't spend it on a woman if it didn't include something he wanted to do! This is an example of a selfish man. You don't need someone like this in your life. He later wrote me an email, begging me to tell him what I didn't like about him. Never a good thing to do—just ignore it. But, at the time, being new at online dating, I told him. But he just didn't get it. They never do. So, don't bother. It will only cause you aggravation and cost you time.

Back to the photos. There are plenty of groupons, social living, or local deals on the Internet for professional photography. So, even if you don't have discretionary income, you can still get good pictures. If you can afford it, I suggest you find someone who does "Boudoir" photos or pin-up girl photos. They are the ones who use that lovely fan that blows your hair around while you are in sexy poses. Seriously, it makes a difference! Look at the magazines. Everybody's hair is wind blown! It's sexy to a guy.

Getting a shoot from a photographer who did this type of photography was one of the best investments I ever made—trust me on this one. You will be thrilled to have an edge over all the other photos online. The photographer will shoot the different sides of you! Sensual, funny, carefree!

All in all, they will make you damn alluring. Many will have outfits for you, or you can bring your own. Have fun with it!! Sexy black dress and heels, babydoll pajamas, corset, stocking, gloves, etc. Let your imagination run wild. Maybe you won't be able to use one or two of those photos online, but you can crop it where you want and use it as a head shot. Plus you get to look at these shots when you're ninety! Blow them up, frame them, and hang them up around your house. You'll feel great about yourself, even on the worst days! Bring items with you that might suggest a hobby. An outfit tells a story. Gardener's cutting shears, wide-brim hat, plaid shirt, pants, apron, chef's hat, holding a glass of wine in one hand and a wooden spoon in the other. However, this may draw the attention of someone who wants to be spanked! OK if you're into it, right?

But, if there is a picture with you holding a wine glass and you really like wine, that is conveyed to the viewer. Alcohol is an important issue to potential mates, one way or the other. Most want to know if you indulge or not.

Bring a hiking outfit—or a swimsuit if you can pull it off body-wise, but don't make it overly sexual. Most photographers know what they are doing and have their own way of getting across what you want the viewer to see. You will see photos online with guys fishing on a boat, wearing a speedo at the beach (OK—maybe they shouldn't, but you will see it), climbing a mountain, riding a bike. A guy wearing a scuba-diving outfit, playing the piano, maybe dancing, pictures of events. It tells a lot about a person, and you will enjoy meeting people of similar interests.

By the way, there is such a thing as having too many pictures. Limit yourself to 7 to 8 good pictures. It's best if you have 4 or 5 pictures that you can mix into your photo profile once in a while.

Every time you add a picture to the site or change the main profile picture, the site will make mention of a picture change, and it usually moves your photo to the front of the line. So mixing your pictures up and changing main photos once a month—at least—works to your benefit. The same thing happens if you edit your profile. It can be important where your picture and profile are placed on the site and how often you go to the front of the line. More about that subject in another chapter. Just remember: Your picture should say something about you.

A big smile shows a happy attitude, or a pose with your hair being blown in the wind can make you seem desirable, fun, and approachable.

Also, you may decide to let a family member take your pictures. I did that early on. Oh, yeah—not a good idea! Your pictures need to have some sex appeal to them. I just couldn't bring myself to purse my lips together or try to pose sexy while my son was taking my pictures. He is a great photographer, but there was no way I was getting anything but nice, motherly pictures from his camera.

Again, a photographer who doesn't know you allows you to be or do whatever you want to. You'll get to put some dreamy eyes or a sexy pose on those photos!

*Again, you'll need great photos of you, **but please be sure they are current!***

CHAPTER FOUR

The Dating Sites

*W*hich site is right for you? In my experience, the largest, most-used site is *match.com*. I've met most of my dates or relationships on this site, and it is the site on which I met *"The Best Husband Ever."* I wasn't looking for a person I could live with. I was looking for the "one" I couldn't live *without*! So it took a lot of effort and time.

But it was worth all the effort, because then came Paul.

Paul and I met one Sunday afternoon for drinks and appetizers, and the conversation rolled in and out so easily. We had a lot in common and laughed a lot about things we did as kids. We were having such a good time. It was easy to see we weren't in a hurry to rush off. But after two hours, we left the restaurant with a goodbye kiss and the promise we would again be talking soon to each other. At that time, I was also starting to see another man, and I wasn't sure which one of the two interested me the most. There were phone conversations with both, and then I went out with each of them again. It was my birthday, so I had birthday dates with both of them.

One of them, Paul, really took the time and energy to stand out. My birthday date with him was really sweet. This was our second date, with maybe two quick phone calls in between, that week. He not only showed up with a lovely birthday card and a dozen red roses, but he even put the roses in a vase for me when he got to my house to pick me up. We had dinner at an Italian restaurant (I offered to make the reservation), and, again, the conversation was off and running. This time our conversation included talk of our families, relationships, and what each of us envisioned our future to look like. Things moved really quickly after that. We both just knew this was it for us! Being in our late sixties, we also knew we had limited time to go through what was left of our lives. We were inseparable after the first two weeks, engaged within two months, and married within four months. We both offered the other what "we knew we needed" to be successful in a new lifetime, and we felt confident that we both could deliver on those needs. We realize how lucky we were to want to continue to make each other happy every day!

I'm a believer in going with your gut instincts. I had also had a lot of experience in dating, and that helped a lot. Again, that's why I say to you: Go out with as many people as you can. It really helps you to realize who will make you happy.

If you are older than 55, other than *match.com*, consider a couple of sites like *OurTime.com* or *seniorpeoplemeet.com*—or any other site that caters to the 55-and-older-crowd. All of these sites charge money to use them. I don't recommend a free site like *plentyoffish.com*. If a person doesn't want to pay for a site to meet someone, then he is just window-shopping for the hell of it.

It is best to invest yourself with a three-month membership on any of the sites. Do not put yourself on "automatic renewal," because it is very difficult to get them to return your money if you want to cancel. Most times, the cost per month of the site will be a lot less for a year, but you may find someone quickly, so a three- or six-month subscription is preferable.

You will see more action, meaning it will be busier on the dating sites at certain times. There will be new profiles or more people contacting each other. October is a busy month as people start thinking about having someone to be with during the holidays—Thanksgiving, Christmas, and then New Year's Eve! People will be looking for that special someone to join them at a family's or friend's holiday table. The months of January and February are also another busy time. People who will want to end a relationship they are in will wait for the holidays to be over to end it. They will then be searching for that special someone to join them for Valentines Day. After that, the site can get very busy with the cooler weather. More people are indoors right through spring. The summer is usually the slowest, as people are outside more or on vacation. So you will see ups and downs on the site during these periods. Take full advantage of this! Spend more time searching.

How to Maneuver Through the Beginning Questions of Your Online Profile

Most people have the hardest time coming up with a head-line. Corny, sensitive, or cute is the key to getting attention when someone sees your picture. First and foremost, think *teethlady*

of a name that will be the name on your profile. It can be a very important piece of information to the men who read it. Make it fun for someone else to read. Clever names work. Something cute like Candygirl, SugarNSpice, Soulmate, Girlygirl, Westernlady, Whiskeymama. It should be short and catchy—no more than 20 letters long.

Pick something that you think describes you or who you are or what you like to do in a fun way. Remember it is a run on words, so be careful what you say. My friend used "fungirlforyou." It turned out not to be a very good profile name. Men thought she just wanted to have a fun time (aka sex). Or, if you *are* looking for sex, then, by all means, use something like that!

I don't suggest you go online to see what the other female profiles use for their names or their written profiles. For one thing, it will show up as a hit on their profile. Secondly, it will confuse you all the more in picking your own profile name and writing your very own profile. Try to think it out on your own.

Filling Out the Profile Questionnaire

*t*he questionnaire will ask personal details regarding your relationship status. Questions such as:

- *Single*, which means that you never have been married.
- *Divorced*, which means that you have already been married.
- *Widow*, which, of course, means that your last mate or companion died.

Children

This is asking whether you have children or want children. If you have them, some sites want to know the age range or number of children.

Income

I don't think this matters a lot to men, but I think every man wants an independent woman. By the way, it is important that you look at *everything* men answer on their profile. When you read someone's profile, it is important to look at their income.

I have found that most men do not lie about their income. If their income is less than $30,000, they are most likely retired, on social security, or have a very limited amount of income for dating. So, you should always be sure that, when you read a profile, you automatically look at the income. Men who enter an income of $150K+ are probably still working and have great 401(k)s. The amount of money that a man enters is basically what he lives on annually. Money may not be an important aspect to you, but you need to be aware of their income, for many reasons. If you don't have regular income or saved income to live on for your "golden years," and if he has none, those years won't be very golden. Plus, you never know who you'll fall in love with. If you can't support yourself and him, it will be more like the "nickel years" for you and him.

Eye and Hair Color

If you absolutely have to have a certain eye color, by all means mark it. If you are between 30 and 40, plan to have children, and want only blue-eyed babies, then it matters.

The same goes for hair. If you want only bald men, so be it.

But remember, this will limit your emails, because if you express too particular a desire, you will not get responses from someone who reads your profile. People take a profile seriously. This area is best to mark ANY. This will give you the greatest responses from the site.

Age

While this is a rather easy process, there are still things to be aware of. Age listing can be a little touchy. It does ask your age, and, at a point, it does ask what age range you are looking for to meet.

Luckily, they don't ask for your weight, but it wouldn't matter. Women would lie about it anyway, just like they lie about their age. And yes, a woman can lie about her age. It is really the only tiny white lie you should have on your profile if you want to show your age as younger or that you have worked at looking young. You can fudge on about 5 to 7 years, as long as you still look it and you still resemble your current picture. It's your call.

Most people know that age is a vehicle for the search engine that is used in online dating sites. You might be 69, but show your age as 64. You can use your search years as 55–65. Most people show a lower age in their search. They don't want to disclose their real age. But most men will not state their search-engine years at 69–79 to look for a woman, no matter how much older they are. If you want to do this but still want to be honest about your age, you can add a disclaimer at the end of your profile, such as "My age is really ____, but I stated a different age due to the merit of search results that most people employ on the sites."

So, let's say that, if you are 60, your search range could be like 59–69 or even 55–65, depending on how you presently look—especially if you have been told you look younger than you are (by people other than family). If you are 64, your range may be 59–69. However, be aware that, most of the time, if men are in their 70s, they are probably going to show their age as being less than 70, usually with an age range of 65–69. FYI, the *match.co*m site lets you put in an "age range" that you're looking for. The *OurTime.com* site, at this time, does not give you that option.

Should a meet try to pin you down on age, he's not for you. He should be interested in you simply as a person. You don't want some 55-year-old guy looking to get himself a kid from a 35-year-old woman.

Religion

It does ask you about your religion and what religions of other profilers you are looking for. This is an important question. If you're religious or have not been brought up in a specific religion, you should enter what is as close to the truth as possible. If you have not been to church or any house of worship for a long time, it is best to choose the box that says "spiritual." This covers a lot of ground.

Ethnicity

Check as many or as few as you like. Checking all boxes in every area will give you more choices and better results.

Smoking

If a guy checks the "occasional smoker" box, it probably means he smokes cigars, cigarettes, or pot once in a while. If you want to meet someone who does smoke for recreational reasons, you might delicately mention it somewhere in your profile. You might say: "420 on Friday or Saturday evening is a lot of fun." "420" is a code-word term people who smoke pot use to tell others that they use marijuana. Whether they are just an occasional user or a daily user is your call. Most people who smoke marijuana occasionally will not use "420" in their profile. So, if you see it listed in a profile, know that they probably smoke marijuana regularly.

Hobbies or Things You Like to Do

This box is usually at the end of your profile, and many people read it marginally, but it does give a person a feel for your likes.

It is a good idea to check as many boxes as you can. For example, checking "wine tasting" gives the potential match info that you drink alcoholic beverages. It is important to state somewhere if you do not drink or that you would prefer not to match up with someone who does.

Checking "Baseball" doesn't necessarily mean you like to play it but that you enjoy watching it as a spectator. This would probably not apply to something like skiing or fishing. Again, the more boxes you check will give you a bigger audience. However, don't check a box unless you have a real interest. If you check "Football," you may meet a guy who is football-crazy, and, if you know little or care nothing about the game, you will have egg on your face.

CHAPTER SIX

What to Say in Your Profile

or "How the Heck Do I Write About Myself?"

*t*his is an area where everyone gets stumped. It can be excruciating to write about yourself without sounding conceited dull, angry, or condescending.

Please remember that online sites are not a place to share your deepest thoughts, past therapy stories, or all the things you believe that makes a relationship successful. Stay away from religious beliefs, political beliefs, and from all the things you don't want in a person. Do not portray yourself as the most wonderful, amazing, accomplished human being in this world. Your accomplishments should not be used to "brag" about yourself in a profile. Your profile should tell a story about you. It should not be a laundry list stating your attributes or your weaknesses.

Keep it light and entertaining, but keep it about you and the things that make you happy. If you do work a lot and that does make you happy, you can say something like, "I spend a lot of hours in my flower shop, but it's a labor of love—one I'd love to share with someone."

If you are an outdoors person, you might write: "You'll find me outside most Saturday mornings on a bike ride with friends" or "Drinking coffee on the patio while reading the morning paper or a good book." Paint a picture of the type of person you are and what you like to do. It makes you interesting and approachable.

The reader has something to grab onto to contact you about. If you say, "I like the mountains," it doesn't give the reader a really good piece of info to respond to. But, if you say, "I love hiking in the Santa Monica Mountains," it not only gives a point of reference, but it also allows the reader to consider asking you to meet them for a hike.

Some things not to write in your opening statement of your profile:

- "I really don't know how to describe or write about myself." OK, most of us can't, but a sentence like this to start with is unimaginative and doesn't draw in the reader to continue on.
- "I asked my friends what they thought about me, and they said _____."
- "My mother says that I am _____."

You might, however, have a very clever opening if you use your dog or cat as the writer speaking about their owner. For instance, your dog might say, "Hi, my name is Rover, and I am Nanci's partner in crime—and, boy, do we get into mischief!" Follow through as if your animal is talking about you, but don't let it be about how pretty or compelling you are to be with. Play it cute and fun. And don't overdo it. A paragraph is enough when it's coming from your animal.

It is good to write your profile about your passions or the things that interest you. You might say you're looking for someone to go out to dinner with or to the movies. A note on that, ladies: Please remember that, if a date is taking you to very expensive restaurants several times in a row, he's looking to have a good time. That does not always mean sex, but, more times than not, that is what he's looking for. So, you need to be realistic.

Keep your profile short—just a few paragraphs. Keep it upbeat and friendly, and try to show a side of you that tells the reader that you are fun and adventurous. If you're not that person, then spin it in a different way. After all, everyone loves to have fun, whatever that means to you. That's the key to a great date that makes them want to have another one right away.

A profile should have some structure. Beginning with who you are, what you like to do, and where you are likely to do it: In the mountains, at the beach, at a horse ranch, taking music lessons, etc. So, for instance, you might write, "Most weekends, you'll find me hiking on the Camarillo trail, taking in nature and its peaceful and beautiful scenery."

It's Fine to Say Things Like:

- "I like a great dinner with a good glass of red wine."
- "I enjoy feeling like a kid again when I'm at the beach, building sand castles."

- "I enjoy spending time with my wonderful family on day trips to the ocean or the mountains, but I really like just being with them and having fun!"
- "Some of my best times are with my dog! Playing fetch a ball or taking him to a dog park or the beach makes me happy!"
- "I enjoy going to church and then Sunday breakfast with friends at my favorite breakfast spot."

So, do you see the difference? Just writing, "I like walking on the beach or playing with my dog or going to church or being with my family" is too generic of a statement and doesn't really give the reader a feeling for who you are. It takes the laundry list out of the "I am" and "I want this." Again, you want to paint a picture of yourself. And sure, it's okay to write in your profile what attributes you may be looking for in a mate. It actually helps to weed out what you don't want. Most men will take what they read as gospel, so be conscious of being too much of a stickler in your likes. You could lose a few good men who might have contacted you but were put off by a statement like, "I only like to go out on weekends." Maybe you do, but don't put it in stone.

Some safe statements that let a guy know what your expectations are for a mate or a date:

- "I like a man who says what he thinks and then follows through on those thoughts."

- "I am looking for a man of intelligence with whom I can have meaningful conversations."
- "It is important to me that you be a romantic guy with an easy way about you and looking for a committed relationship or life partner."
- "I'm hoping you'll be a straight shooter and tell it like it is—someone who loves his family and friends but is looking to extend his love to a woman, and not just with words."

In my experience, I have found that most profiles men write are pretty honest and as truthful as they appear to be. Some men will write too little or too much about themselves or interests. If he writes too little, he's not putting a lot of effort into finding "the one." He is basically shopping for a date. If he writes way too much in his profile, he is most likely self-absorbed and thinks the more you know about him, the more impressed you'll be.

Look for a cleanly written profile that doesn't have any negativity about it—either openly or between the lines. Many times, you will see a comment like, "My posted pictures are current. Please do the same and post current photos of yourself. It is only fair play." Now, that's an OK comment. It's genuine and yet informative.

Remember: A woman lies about her age online, while most men may lie about their height. To me, that doesn't matter as long as the height is within a few inches and the woman's age is within a few years. A man may put his height a couple of inches higher, and it is not unusual if he is shorter. I never minded it when I met a guy who said he's 5'8" but is really 5'6". Height is not something a person can change. However, pictures that are 10 years older or more are not fair to anyone. No one looks the same 10 years later. So be prudent about that, and "play fair."

CHAPTER SEVEN

Writing Your Profile

*t*his is not a therapy page or a session with your counselor. It is not a place to tell everyone what you did wrong in your relationships and how much you learned. You do not want to tell everyone you have now learned what makes a great relationship and proceed with a list.

The way to go about writing a profile is to have a structure. There are a lot of ways to do that, but, realistically, you want to start with who you are, what you like to do, and the type of person you're looking for. Therefore, to help you get started quickly, I want to give you a template to fill in. You can embellish it and change it around at another time, but at least it will help get you started on what to write, which is the hardest part. You will at least get yourself online quickly.

Potential First Paragraph for Your Opening
"If you're looking for me, you'll probably find me

_____.

(Fill in the blank)

Examples:

"Hiking to the very top of a mountain"

"Walking my dog, Spot"

"Traveling a long way to work on the 405"

"Having fun with my family and/or grandkids"

"At the gym" or "In the kitchen" or "In the garden"

"Sitting in the park 'people-watching'"

"In a forest, enjoying the beauty and quiet while watching the squirrels frolic"

You get the idea. Place yourself in a setting you're most likely to be at.

Now, if you are a major shopper, I suggest it is best to say something like "antiquing" or "roaming antique stores." While every woman generally likes to shop, I don't suggest putting that into your profile. Men see the word "shopping" and automatically think of their money being spent. I know that sounds ridiculous. Please don't shoot the messenger. It's just true.

Second Paragraph in Your Profile: Your Likes

It's a good place to tell a story about the things you like in life. In the examples below, the fill-ins are for you to figure out. Think about you and your thoughts.

"I am a lover of classical music and movies. My favorite movie/musician is _____."

"There's something about a(n) _____ (favorite snack) that really makes me smile."

"Give me that with a _____ cold beer, root beer, or glass of milk, and I'm a happy camper!!

Although I do love _____

_____."

Examples:

A funny movie.

Two-stepping at the Borderline Club.

A 10-mile bike ride.

Driving my car with the top down (not *my* top down).

Volunteering at the Humane Society.

Volunteering at my local hospital.

Volunteering at the Four Oaks Wine Bar.

You get the idea—right? If you can add some humor, do it. Everyone needs to read a chuckle. Also it is OK to show that you still enjoy intimacy and romance, as some women do not. You might write:

"I like the genuine intimacy of a man and woman together. I believe it is an important aspect of life and romance. Plus . . . it's a hell of a lot of fun, too!"

Or "Romance and intimacy go together. There is no substitute for the closeness of a man and woman when they share a kiss . . . or three."

Potential Third Paragraph (This should be the final one!)

You don't want to go on and on about yourself, for two reasons. First, the reader will get bored and not bother to finish reading it, and the important stuff might be at the end of your profile. Secondly, you don't want tell too much about yourself too early on.

At this point in your profile, you should have given the impression of what you like to do and the kind of person you are. By the second paragraph, you should have given the reader a good idea of your likes about books, movies, music, food, hobbies, etc. If you have a passion for something, this is a good place to mention it.

The third paragraph is the one where you describe the type of person you're looking for. Remember: We all have a type and qualities we really want to find in a mate. If you don't know what this is, you need to do some deep thinking. It helps the reader decide if you might be for him.

Template for Third Paragraph:

Here is a template to fill in. Use one or more—but not all—of the suggested phrases.

"I'm hoping that you _____.**"**

"Are a standup guy!"

"Possess a good wit."

"Are a person of integrity."

"Like telling a good story."

"Have the ability to laugh at yourself!"

"Really want to be in love."

"Are looking for a meaningful relationship."

"Love spending time with family."

"Are empathetic toward others."

"Are not judgmental."

"Have an open mind."

"Like to travel."

"Love long car trips."

"Love dogs." "Love cats."

OR "Hoping that you're _____ **"**
"Not afraid of commitment."
"Financially secure."
"Nurturing and caring of others."
"Respectful of others' opinions and ideas."
"Adaptable and willing to compromise."

One last thing: _Don't write about what you_ don't _want in a person._
Some men and women who have been dating online a long time have felt betrayed by photos or profiles that were not honest or current. Some write paragraphs that say exactly what they _don't_ want in a person. I call them "disclaimers." Most people will stop being interested in a person's profile when it becomes negative in attitude and spirit. I have read disclaimers at the end of the profile that say:

"If you're just looking for a free dinner, please don't write me."

"If your pictures are 15 years younger than you are now, please don't contact me."

"I don't want drama in my life, so, if you're a drama queen, pass me by."

"If you're still in love with your ex, don't email me."

"If you're just looking for a sugar daddy, I'm not for you."

"Please don't come with a lot of baggage. A suitcase or two is OK."

Again, these types of comments are negative, written by people who have experienced frustration from their previous dating experiences. Maybe they are looking for the wrong things in people to make them happy and/or have been burnt too often by bad picks. However, if you want to use some kind of disclaimer, try something like this—but use it at the *very end* of your profile:

"BTW: If you don't look like your picture when we meet, you're buying me drinks until you do!"

This brought a lot of smiles to a lot of people when I put it on my profile.

I have had many men email me about this line. They say, "I don't fit your profile criteria, but that is the funniest line I have ever read in anyone's profile! I just had to tell you that—maybe over drinks?"

And, you gotta love the guy who wrote me: "I would really love to meet you, and I'll buy you drinks until you like what I look like."

As a reference for how to write your profile, I have included some sample profiles at the back of this book. These are examples to give you an idea of what and how you might convey yourself—a snapshot of who you are and what you are looking for in a person.

CHAPTER EIGHT

What Am I Looking For—Really?

*i*f a person writes, "Looking for someone to share my life with" compared to someone who writes, "Looking for someone to hang out with," well, that should tell you something. One definitely shows commitment, while the other does not. And you *should* know what you're looking for. What type of man do you want in your life? Try to think about your experiences in the past that haven't worked out. Maybe you just picked the wrong type of person to complement you.

The laws of attraction say that you attract what you project. Most times, that's true, but many people do have a *type* that they look for. Do you attract bad boys? Boring men? Egotistical men? Sports jocks? Maybe your attraction is based solely on looks or financial status. Think about what your "type" is when you're looking at profiles online.

We all have a type, and you should know what type of person you find most attractive. If you have not been successful in finding what type has worked for you, then maybe you will have to adjust your type and pick men differently. Are you picking people who are wrong for you? Are you, your-self, giving out the positive traits to others that you expect from them?

What you are attracted to may not be the best person for you to stay happy with. That is one of the reasons you should go out with **people whom you normally would not date. You will be surprised at the outcome.** Remember that opposites attract, but like minds stay together! I have gone on a lot of first meets where I knew that they were really not my type. Even though I thought, *This is going to be a boring meet,* I was really surprised quite a few times. While they weren't what I thought was "my type," I was attracted to their personalities and their ideas. It changed my perspective about who I was really looking for. (Although, I knew it could never be the guy who had so much nose hair that it looked like his nose had a mustache attached to it. Oh, yeah—I had one of those. I couldn't look at him while he spoke. It was too painful.)

So, you will find some of them boring, too talkative, too loud, too aggressive, or just too polite! They will have really large ears, a scraggly goatee, a large mole on their face, be too tall, too short, too muscular, or too scrawny. You will find the guy who will take you to lunch or dinner and wants to tell the waiter not only his name but yours, too—just so friendly! Uh, huh. Personally, I don't like it when that happens to me. I don't think our server needs to know my name, and I really don't need to know where the server lives or that he has lived in California or where they go to school or work, or how their brother just went into the service. Please believe, I am interested in people's lives, but at a time like this, especially on a first meet, it should just be about the two of you getting to know each other quickly—kind of like speed dating. If he is trying to show you what a great guy he is by engaging everyone around you, it says something about him. Maybe he's just a little too egotistical, or maybe he's trying just a little too hard to be liked. Honestly, to me, it's a turnoff, and, sometimes, I find it to be a red flag. It's the same thing that's going on when someone talks over you while you're trying to finish a sentence. It usually means he thinks what he has to say is much more important or funny than what you have to say.

While I have patience, I don't think I want my first date to give me a lecture about which planets are revolving around me at this very moment. I don't need to be impressed by his scientific knowledge of our atmosphere or a 2-minute dissertation on why I *should* be watching *The Walking Dead*. I'm not saying you shouldn't share everyday moments in life, but it should be just a reference of the type of shows or movies that one watches so we can see if we are compatible in those areas.

Is he boring you to death? Let's hope that it doesn't happen to you. Certainly, you should be careful that you're not the one doing the boring. If it does happen to you on a meet, gently try to change the subject or point out something unusual you see around you. Then, don't let him get right back to it with, "Oh, where were we?" Change the subject quickly.

Look, everyone comes with baggage. Find someone who loves you enough to help you unpack.

CHAPTER NINE

OK—Are You Ready to Go Searching?

Think of it as shopping—one of my favorite things to do.

*Y*ou should now be prepared, with the questionnaire filled out, your profile written, and beautiful pictures of you up on the site. If you're on a site like *Match.com* or *OurTime.com*, you've set up your account with them and made a payment with a credit card. The site will approve your profile and photos to be sure there is nothing inappropriate about your photos or language (full or partial nudity or profanity). Also, they do not want you to put your email address in your profile, for safety reasons. This process may them take up to 24 hours. You may use the option "hide my profile" if you are not ready to go online and start receiving emails. The "hide my profile" can also be used if you go away on vacation and don't want contact from other site members or if you start dating a new meet somewhat seriously and want to see where it goes. It will not show your profile and will state that ". . . the profile of this person is not available."

When you do become active, you will receive a lot of "hits" (flirts or emails) immediately from people already on the site. There are different ways to search for people, and there is an option you can use to show you only the new people who come onto the site. This is usually for people who have been on the site quite a while and want to see only the "fresh blood" (new profiles) that comes on the site. Some people have been on these same sites for years. They will most likely have the option set for the "new members."

OK, so now you're online and ready to roll. Exciting stuff!!!

When you start receiving these flirts and you're interested, flirt back. If you're really interested, send an email back. Just a few lines will do.

Pick out something in their profile, and use that in the body of an email. For instance, if they write that they like to hike in the Santa Monica Mountains, maybe you can write, "I like to hike the Santa Monica hills, also. Where do you go afterwards to quench your thirst? I usually go to _____."

This gives them the opportunity to email back with, "Hey, why not meet there Saturday morning?" It is best to give someone you'd like to meet an opening. This makes it easier for them to ask you to meet. You'll find most guys do not want to email someone more than a couple of times. Sometimes, in their profile, they will state, "I'm not looking for a pen pal." This means they want to meet people quickly to see if there is a spark. This is actually the best way to go about dating online.

After a couple of emails that look promising, take the lead if he doesn't, and ask him to meet you for a drink or a coffee. Offer him a set day and time—morning if you want to meet for coffee or evening if you want to meet for a drink. Personally, I found that, if I was unsure about my interest in meeting someone, I'd make a meet for coffee, because it usually is half an hour or so. But, if I thought I might really like him, I'd offer to meet him for a drink in the evening. I found evening meets with a glass of wine to be a lot more relaxed, and there is more potential for a next date. Hey—everyone looks good in dim lighting!

When you're the one setting up the meet, don't make it a Saturday night. Save that for a second or third date. If it's a Monday, try to set it up for Wednesday, two days later. Making meets online needs to be quick. Two days is good, because it's not the next day (too soon) or the third day (too much time in between). Strike while the iron is hot, and don't leave a lot of wiggle room for someone else online to get the meet first. Chances are that, if you make a meet for the following week, and it's after the weekend, it's probably going to be cancelled. Someone else will pique either his or your interest during that time. Because, if you were both really interested in meeting each other, one of you would have set up a quick meet—within a day or two.

Hopefully, you are emailing with guys who live within a 10-mile radius. You should look as locally as possible for your meets. Older men do not like to date more than 15–20 minutes away. Night-vision driving, traffic, drinking and driving (DUI) is a worry for all of us mature people.

By the way, the guys who want to meet you on a Friday or Saturday night who live 45 minutes to an hour away are planning an overnight stay at your place. You may say, "No way," but if they say they're too looped or too tired to drive, you have options. They can sleep it off on your couch if your gut feels they're harmless, or you can call Uber to take him to the nearest hotel. It's a good idea if you know what the closest hotel is and Uber's number. So, dating local makes a lot of sense, doesn't it?

CHAPTER TEN

Setting Up the Meet

*i*f you can avoid it, I do suggest you meet without a phone conversation. But, if you or they would rather have a phone conversation before meeting, then ask for his number, so you can control the time and place you call him from. Also ask him, "What is the best time for you to chat?" That will help him to be in the right place to be available for an uninterrupted conversation with you. If he says, "You can call me in the evening after 8 PM," then give him a response about the exact date and time you will call.

If you say you're going to call him Sunday at 8:15 PM, make sure you do call him at that time and not 20 minutes or half an hour later. Men appreciate punctuality. It shows respect for their time, and you come off as a lady who is genuine. There needs to be no games played on this. Be a straight shooter, and they will respect you.

Be sure you keep a schedule with the times you are supposed to call and his name. Best to have their profile printed in front of you. This will help you to know who you are calling so you get their name and information right. It can be confusing if you have a few different calls to make. And, if you're working hard at this, you *should* have a few to make. I once called a guy and spoke with him for about five minutes and realized he was not the guy I was supposed to have called at that specific time. Uh, oh! Heart-pounding moment! Luckily, I didn't stay on the phone with him for more than a few minutes.

I have also forgotten to call someone when I said I would. The best thing to do if this happens is to just be honest and text them something like, "I'm so sorry. I must have been in a fog yesterday and just forgot our arranged time."

Some guys will say, "I must not be so important if you forgot me!" Just tell him, "It's not you, it's me." If they push it, screw them. I don't mean literally.

But, it just tells you the guy likes to be a power head. He likes to give people guilt trips, and it's most likely that he enjoys seeing people squirm. That means he likes to have the upper hand. Seriously, do you need someone like that in your life? Go on to someone else! A real gentleman and a good guy will say, "No problem. I've had those days, too."

If you're pushed to have a phone conversation, keep it to the 10-minute rule, and don't ask a lot of questions about them or their family. You can talk about restaurants, hobbies—nothing personal. If they ask you a lot of questions, tell them you would rather meet someone first before you divulge a lot of personal info. After all, these are complete strangers. They don't need to know your life story or why you're single and looking, so don't feel bad about not answering what they might think is a common question. You do not need to pacify others who are curious. Just smile and go on to something else. "Do you work?" is a question they might ask you so they can possibly determine a meet time. That's OK! If they ever, casually or jokingly, ask your income or talk dollars and cents, just tell them you work for the IRS. That usually shuts them up!

Keep the conversation light. After a few minutes of talking to each other, he might say to you, "We should meet sometime!" If you are also interested in meeting him, by all means, make the move. You can say something like "I can meet you for a drink after work on Tuesday around 7 PM. How does that work for you?" Intrigue him, but that's all. If he tells you he is not sure, as he has to check his work schedule or whatever but does not give you a possible alternate day or time to meet you, forget him. He's not interested in you. If he was, he would be hammering a definite date and time to meet you. He wouldn't put you off.

Shouldn't he be excited to meet you? You bet he should!

So, should he falter about setting up a meet, then just say to him, "Hey—no problem. Nice talking with you!" and hang up. Seriously—just thank him, and hang up! He just wants to know everything about you to gauge if you are worth his time or his money for cocktails. Don't play the game with him.

He might call you back and say something such as, "Listen, I really want to meet you, but I don't have my calendar in front of me." Tell him again, "No problem. But, text or email me when you know your schedule, and I'll see what mine looks like, also." That's it! Do not belabor the conversation.

He either wants to meet you, or he doesn't. The ball is in his court! Let him cross the line to you!

Have a few places ready to give as a meeting place. Hopefully, you've done your homework. There is nothing worse than saying, "Oh, gosh. I don't know" about where to meet.

Remember: You choose the spot and, believe it or not, they actually like that they don't have to decide. If you need reservations, tell them you will be happy to make them. You're showing them your contribution to the date. Also, if you make the reservation, you can ask for a certain table, maybe one you know is conducive to having a quiet conversation, without a lot of distractions. Then, make those reservations through the Internet on "Open Table." That way, you even get to keep the points they give you for each reservation made with them. After so many reservations, they send you a $25 gift certificate to use at the restaurants they show on their site. You might as well get the $25 to eat with a friend or family member. Hey—it's a win-win!

And, please remember:

The purpose of the phone call should be to make a date to meet for a drink or coffee.

End of story!

CHAPTER ELEVEN

Get Ready to Meet Your Match, but Be Prepared!

ost women's first worry is what to wear for a meet. The more prepared you are to go on first meets, the more confident you'll become. You will be relaxed and able to focus on the meet with him and not about how you look. Most times, you'll wonder if he finds you attractive. This is a common thought. But, turn it around, as it's not about what he likes. *You need to like him!* Put yourself first.

When you meet someone, if you are comfortable in how you look, what you're saying, and at the place you're saying it, he will become relaxed and show you more of his true self. You will come off as a "confident in your own skin" woman. So how do you get to that point? *Here is your homework assignment.*

Have a few ready-to-go outfits together. I call them "clothes vignettes."

Put together a full outfit or two. I mean dress heels, purse, sweater/jacket, the right undergarments for the outfits that you know you can put together quickly and that you feel sexy and confident wearing. Test the outfits out in a supermarket. (Trader Joe's or Whole Foods is a good one.) If you are getting a few good head-turns from men, then that's a date outfit!

For coffee or lunch meets, I suggest you wear either a casual skirt and top or jeans and casual top or tee shirt. Sneakers, sandals, or boots are acceptable, too.

For a drink in the evening, a dress solves the problem of putting an outfit together. Keep some stock clothes for first meets. A couple of nice, easy, casual dresses. You can wear them over and over again for new meets. This way, you won't have to think about what you should wear. If you meet for drinks, I suggest you wear heels with a dress if you can. Men love dresses and heels. 2", 3", or 4" heels—the size of the heel doesn't matter. But, not a wedge heel, a slim heel. It matters. Most wedge heels won't interest a guy. And, they do notice your shoes if it's got a slim heel. I'm just saying!

Go easy on the makeup. A lot of blush or contour makeup just looks fake. I've heard many men talk about a date on which the woman's makeup was so overdone that it kinda turned them off. Guys like a fresh-looking face. Men are basically looking for "the girl next door," with some sexiness thrown into the mix. Keep it as natural as you can.

Write down the items you put together on a list, or take a photo of yourself in a full-length mirror, so you'll remember the outfit again and have all the items readily available when the time comes. It will help you feel calmer and happier instead of nervous or anxious, because you will know exactly what you're going to wear.

And, I strongly suggest you don't wear anything low cut on a first meet. After a first meet, whatever feels comfortable to you is fine, but if you're looking for a serious relationship, cover up that décolletage. Let them guess what's going on under there. It will also help them to keep their eyes on your face and not on your chest. The conversation will go more smoothly and be more meaningful for both of you!

Next, you should have two or three restaurants you are comfortable visiting for a meet. This also gives you a quick answer when the decision of where to meet is left to you. You should be the one to decide where, if he is any kind of a considerate gentleman. It should be ladies' choice, and remember: You don't do the traveling. He comes to you! That means you should scout out a couple of restaurants close to where you live. Bar/restaurants are really good spots to meet. It doesn't assume you will have dinner together, but it does give you the opportunity to say "Yes" to dinner if you're hungry and like him, or "Sorry. I have plans for later," should he ask you to stay and have dinner there. Most times, I have found that the two of you will more than likely have appetizers while you're drinking and chatting. That is the best way to handle a first meet. Eat some food while you drink.

When scouting out restaurants of your choice, order a glass of wine and possibly an appetizer or even something from the dinner menu while you are there. You don't want to be too fussy when you order what you drink or eat at the actual meet.

The ability to quickly order your drink or even an appetizer will make you seem confident, instead of the girl who says "Gee, I don't know. What are you having?"

Consider it a dry run, a plan for a meet. If you have preplanned this part of the meet, you will be able to concentrate on what your date has to offer in the way of conversation, attitude, and manners. If you're not too preoccupied thinking about you or your surroundings, you will come off as a cool, confident lady, and the conversations between the two of you will flow more easily. This will put both of you at ease. You will be in a better position to get a handle on what he's all about pretty quickly.

For a coffee meet, pick a place that is not too small. In other words, you want to converse, but don't make it such a small place that your conversation is overheard by everyone. It will make you uncomfortable. If you want to meet for coffee, meet at a Starbucks or a Coffee Bean or Peet's.

I always went to the same two or three restaurants on a first meet. While the staff there knew I was in there a couple of times a week—and always with a different guy—they never let on that they were familiar with me. So, don't get chummy with the help at these places, especially at the bar area. Just be cordial. You don't need to be seen as a regular who brings their meets there for a "romance interview." And they should be happy to get the business from you.

It is best if you meet your date outside or at the front of the restaurant or coffee shop, instead of sitting in a bar/coffee place and hoping he recognizes you.

Don't make it awkward and difficult for your meet. Remember, you both are looking at lots of pictures. It is not unusual that a man will walk up to another woman in the bar and ask her if she's you. Just meet outside. He'll know it's you. (Well, unless you use a 10-year-old picture or you've gained 20 pounds. *That's a no-no!*)

If, by chance, you think you are so charming that you'll hope he'll forget that you don't look like your picture, well, you're not—and he won't. He will feel duped. You would, too, if it happened to you.

Also, do not meet in a place that makes you think about happy memories of you and your ex or someone you still yearn for. It will make you think about how much you're still in love with your ex if the meet is a disappointment. Don't set yourself up to fail!!

So, plan ahead. Knowing exactly what you'll be wearing, where you're going, and what you'll order can make a big difference at a meet. Always remember to have a big smile on your face when meeting your date! After all, you are his guest. He's paying for you to be there!

Consider yourself in a play. Know your costumes, your lines, and your stage. If you're not thinking about how you look, how you hold your glass or eat your food, it won't be about you. It will be about him and how you really perceive him.

Having a set conversation and questions, a few cute stories about you or your escapades to share with your meet will lead you through the acts of the play! Just like having a few different outfits to wear, a fun conversation will help you to be comfortable and confident. Confidence will let your date see you genuinely for who you are. Whether you two click or not, you will feel good about how things went. Also, be careful you don't make all these dates your new "best friends" or "friends with benefits." Remember, that is not your goal. You can get those kind of friendships pretty much anywhere. Your insecurities are the roadblocks to you enjoying your date! Just as salespeople are trained on their products, they also know how perform while giving the product demonstrations. That's what makes them better than their competition. Your product is you. Learn about you and how you can outperform your competition in the dating world. That will be the way you will achieve the confidence in yourself that you need to have fun at your meet.

That's why I tell you the more people you go out to meet, the better you will become at first, second, and third dates.

Investing in Yourself

Remember to invest in yourself. It is extremely important for you to feel great about yourself when you are competing in the dating world at any age—but, in reality, it gets harder as we get older.

If your teeth are yellow or missing, get them fixed even if you have to put it on a credit card. The same goes for a scar, acne, sun damage, or strongly wrinkled skin. There are laser and other procedures today that can be a tremendous help to how you feel and look. Some of them are costly, but if you are on a budget or don't have discretionary income, there are some no- or low-interest credit cards for cosmetic or dental surgery available at some physicians' offices. Many of them even offer a monthly payment plan. Why not look into it?

Maybe you give up a Starbucks coffee every day, bring your lunch from home, or eat sandwiches for dinner. Investing in yourself in the places on your body that bother you will be so worth it in the long run in many ways. If that means you need to lose a few pounds, go walking! It's free, and you will lose weight and firm up with just 30 minutes a day of good, brisk walking. The changes you make will radiate confidence.

Look good, feel good, and you'll do good!

CHAPTER TWELVE

How to Give Good Emails

*t*here are times when you just don't know what to say or how to approach someone in an email. It really helps if you have a list of opening one-liners that are, funny, interesting, and, especially, questioning. You want the recipient to be compelled to write you back. I know how hard it can be to reach out to someone and sound cute or witty or interesting. So I'm giving you a few lines as examples so you get the idea—lines that you can put in the subject line of your email. Try to make it somewhat exciting, maybe with a little come-on so the person is eager to open it. It's men-shopping, remember? All of these should be followed with the email that's connected to it somehow. Remember: These are only opening subject lines.

(Subject line) You blew me away!
(Email body) when I read you climbed Mount Whitney!

(Subject line) The best part of today
(Email body) would be your hello

(Subject line) You wow'd me
(Email body) with your escapades in _____ (Africa,
   fishing, etc.)

(Subject line) It's a little bit funny that our profiles
(Email body) almost mirror each other in the things we
   love to do!

Subject line) Imagine if we met . . .
(Email body) at that place in Mexico you wrote about

(Subject line) Superglued lips?
(Email body) Not too much info in your profile.
   Hmmm. Are you with the CIA?

The best email I ever received was: "You're so hot that,
when I looked at your pictures, you melted my computer!"
That's a clever opening line. I laughed so hard because it was so
funny, and everyone wants to think they're hot! I was not really
attracted to his photo, but I thought he was so witty that I was
compelled to write him back. This opened it up for a few fun
email conversations with him, and it did lead to a phone call.
Nice guy, and I thought he'd be a fun friend to have, but he just
lived too far away. Also, there are always a few guys you meet
who really just want to be friends—some "with benefits." No
matter what a man's age is, he, like you, likes to think he's hot!

If these opening lines seem like come-ons—they are! You want that person to write you back to at least start a conversation. Again, these are marketing approaches to get his interest going. Think of it as kind of a mini-commercial. You're just looking to get their attention. There is nothing wrong with putting together a few opening lines and using them over and over again with different profilers.

This is one reason I tell you to email as many guys as you can. But be sure you know who is who and what you said to each of them. Keep notes. In my experience, it's the numbers of contacts you make that lead to the ratio of meets. I've found that it usually works out to a 1% ratio if you spend the time. For every 50 flirts you send, you should get about 4–5 good emails back from the pool of profiles, which will get you to meet at least one of those emails. Maybe two if you are open to meeting almost anyone, within reason. If you are too fussy, your man ratio will drop. You can be fussy on the second date, not the first date.

Does this sound like a lot of work? It is!

Everyone can make time for an hour out of the day to work at finding the love of your life! The more you work at this, the easier it gets. Your goal is to find the person who can keep you interested enough for a third or fourth date. Otherwise, move onward and forward. When you are in your golden years, you don't have the luxury of being wrong over a long term. The more people you meet, the better your odds are for meeting a mate. Consider it a sales job. You have to contact a lot of people to find an interested buyer. Only hard work, perseverance, tenacity, and knowledge of your product will get you the meets you will need to be successful at this. *You* are the "product." Know what you're worth.

Remember: Don't get disheartened. Don't give up. You gotta believe to make it happen. And it will happen!

CHAPTER THIRTEEN

Red Flags

*W*hat is a red flag? If you think someone is not genuine in his search, he probably isn't!

So you need to be diligent about reading between the lines. Not so much that you don't give someone a chance, but just a chance. One email or one meet will usually tell you if he is worth your time.

Some red flags to look out for in men's profiles:

He gives all his very important qualities! He will go on and on about his prowess as a chef or even in the bedroom. Lately, it seems there is a dating world of chefs. There was one profile I read, loaded with many actual recipes in it! It was so long I had to stop for lunch to even go back to reading it! Seriously, it wasn't that he went to the "Chef Cordon Bleu School for Cooking." He just had a large ego. I actually met this guy. And yes, it was just as I thought: Big ego. Steer away from profiles that are very long and go on and on. You actually get exhausted from just reading it. Also, stay away from the very, very short profiles as well—I mean like one paragraph.

There are lots of other red flags to look for:

"I have learned how people should act in a relationship." He will describe to you all he knows about "respect, closeness, and communicating with someone in an honest and meaning-ful way which will only grow you and help you to become a better person." Look out! This guy's had a lot of marriage and therapy counseling. And thinks he could hang his own shingle on a door saying "Ph.D." I have found that he will most likely be a controlling guy who will want to counsel you on "how to have a strong relationship." Because of his many years of counseling, he believes he feels very sure about what your relationship should be. Even in his profile, he writes like a therapist. So, unless he *is* a therapist, and maybe even then, he may be difficult to live with, and he will always believe he is right. Beware this type. Unless, of course, you think you could use him for free counseling. There's always that!

And then . . .

There is the profile that boasts about his three homes (one is always on the ocean), his boat, his collection of classic cars, and his friendships with famous people. He is a name dropper. Money makes this man. He is using it to bait you. Men know that women look for "well to do" men. Yes, most women do want a standup guy who has integrity, but they also look at the dollar signs. Let's be real here. I am not saying you shouldn't go after this type, but if all you are reading about is what this guy has, then, more than likely, that's all he's about. He is casting out the fishing line to see what bites. He is aware of the barracudas and knows how to reel them in and then throw them back when he doesn't want them any longer. Most likely, he has a stable of girlfriends who keep him supplied in the romance area—all of them thinking they're going to be the prize fish.

No matter how wonderful he says you are, there are others on his radar. It is up to you to decide whether you do or don't mind being one of his "actions." I'm not saying it's wrong. If you're seriously looking for Mr. Right, and if you are real and genuine in your search, you will find a real and genuine guy. Laws of attraction at work!

On a serious note about online dating: While I have not had any seriously crazy guys email me, there have been some who I am sure are scams and some who are from other countries, looking for money. Usually, you will see telltale signs. Their spelling and their writing have a lot of errors in it. Delete this immediately. Some will write over and over. If that happens, forward it to the site's customer service. They want to know about it.

Also, I have found the exact same profile on the same site with different names. This is a no-no on dating sites. Customer Service will bar someone from their site if they know about it. If you see this, flag this to the customer service department of that site, and let them handle it.

Police, who handle this type of deception, offer these red flags for online dating scams:

- Examine profile pictures and question if they may have been stolen from another, unrelated site.
- Compare profile pictures to listed physical descriptions to see if they match.
- Closely review profile pictures for small details, such as wedding rings.
- Ask a series of questions over an extended period of time. Watch for inconsistencies in answers.
- Note that many male scammers list their occupations as "engineer" and many female scammers list theirs as "model."
- Conduct online research to confirm that the information you find matches what is listed in the person's profile.
- Ask specific questions about locales in the other person's listed city, and confirm they match their profile.
- Be wary of online daters who ask to communicate by other online means—a common tactic used by scammers.
- Check spelling, grammar, and sentence structure in profiles; there may be tell-tale signs that the person may be communicating from another country, feigning close proximity.
- Never send sexually explicit or compromising images, which can be used as leverage in an extortion attempt.
- Be wary of online daters who become affectionate or serious too soon, including the use of pet names such as "Babe," "Sweetie," "Hon," and "Love."
- Be wary of grandiose stories such as princes in other countries who fall in love online and wish to spend their inheritance on people they don't know.
- Do not send money or gift cards, or wire money transfers.

Now while, these things can happen, it is you who makes a decision about a meet. If it doesn't seem right to you, trust your gut on these things, and move on. Some of the people will be obvious, especially the ones who show bad English and spelling throughout their profile. But, don't be *so* suspicious that you ask too many questions. Most of the people you meet will be just guys looking for the same thing you are. They want to find "the one" and have love in their heart.

CHAPTER FOURTEEN

Where Did All the Men Go?

*t*here are plenty of single men who are online dating, but sometimes it will seem lean on the sites, and then, at other times, it will seem overwhelming. It's just the way it goes on the dating sites! Either every guy on the site is contacting you, or you hear nothing at all. There are going to be times when you wonder, "Where the hell did everyone go? No one is sending me flirts or emails!" There are a couple of reasons this happens—at least, this has been my take on it. Sometimes a lot of new people join the site at once, and, so, the playing field is larger. New people join the site and are advanced to the head of the class picture- or profile-wise by the site (*Match.com, OurTime.com*). So, your flirt or email action decreases a little on the site when many newbies join that site. Your profile may be showing up at the end of the site pages. If you really want attention, run your upgrade (these are the extra hours you buy to get noticed and to be in front) twice a day for a couple of days straight. They are very inexpensive.

Start on Wednesdays or Thursdays. Most men are thinking of weekend dates around that time.

Also vary your site times. Everyone wants the 4, 5 or 6 PM showings, so there will be more profiles up, and you'll be *less visible*. Use your hour run at different times of the day. There's a whole lot of older men who get on at 6 AM or 8 PM You need to know the ups and down of online dating and realize it's not you—it's just the nature of the site. One thing is for certain: You should look forward to getting on the sites daily and as much as you can. It's hard work. Believe me: You can spend 1–2 hours searching or writing emails to people. But, it works if you do it daily! I don't suggest you get on the chat option. You can be chatting with one or ten people at the same time. It is time consuming, and I find that the people who do it a lot are long-distance or just bored and want to talk to a female. Don't waste your time!! Checking out guys' profiles and sending or answering emails results in a better percentage of good meets.

With that said, don't email a person more than twice. Maybe he just skimmed over your first email, so, if you're really interested, write him: "Hi, again. Just wondering if you received my email." If you don't get a response, just move on, and assume that he's just not into you or he has a girlfriend already and just playing online. Many men look at profiles as soft porn.

They look at the pictures only. Be wary if a guy specifies meeting you at times that **never** include a weekend day or night. Be wary of someone who doesn't want to meet you in your area who or wants to meet you in your area at a

certain time or a certain day "just because he is going to be there anyway" for one reason or another. This is for his convenience only. If he asks you to drive halfway to meet him because you live far apart, pass on it. If he lives that far away, you won't see him much, anyway, and you probably wouldn't know if he already has a girlfriend or wife where he lives. If it seems off, it probably is. After all, it is their job to come to you, and they should ask *you* where *you* want to meet. Don't be the playmate. Keep yourself directed toward the goal of meeting "the one" and falling in love. Don't get hung up with the players. Don't get used. It will bring you down when you find out you were being used, and it will just make you quit online dating. Don't let them make you feel that way.

Things No One Will Tell You

Practice dating guys you may not normally want to meet or be interested in. It will be your learning ground—and it may surprise you! Sometimes, it's the one you don't think you'll be interested in who will turn out to surprise you the most! Nice guys really do get overlooked.

By the way, you should also be aware of what the Internet says about you. Google your name. Look yourself up in the white pages. Use your number for reverse finds. Unfortunately, that is what dates will do if they have your number, and most guys will ask for your number before you meet and use the "just in case something comes up" excuse. I just ask for theirs, in case I'm running late, which I make sure doesn't happen. That's acceptable to do, and no one ever seemed to mind that I asked for it. I don't give them mine back. If they ask for it, I don't give it to them right away. I stall and will text it to them an hour or so before the meet for the "just in case something comes up" possibility. They may try to look you up then, but it doesn't really matter at that point.

While I think you should look yourself up and know what it says about you online, I don't suggest you look up your date by name or phone number if you have it. Most people don't look themselves up or know what's been written about them. It may be true or untrue. It's best to know only what is written in their profile. Otherwise, you will prejudge him or slip up and say something you've already read about him on a search. I think it just keeps things fair. A person will tell you what they want you to know—and that's their privilege, just as it is yours.

Also, if you don't want your age or phone number listed on white pages or sites like *Checkmate.com* or one of the locator sites you may have used in the past, you need to take action. Please understand, when you look for information on others, they capture your information, so you need to email the site you have previously used. Call them or write them, and demand that they take you off their list and not show your information. You have the right to privacy. It will sometimes take a few weeks for your removal, so you should do it right away—before you even get yourself onto another site.

Many years ago, I had to call a company and tell them I was being stalked by someone because they had listed so much info about me. OK, yes. It was a small lie. But you need to make them realize that they have an obligation to protect the privacy of the people they use to make their money from.

A rule of thumb is that your date should look like themselves 90% of the time.

Yes, 10% of the time, you'll need to chalk it up to the process. But remember, you will meet all kinds of people, and everyone has a story. Hopefully they won't want to tell you their whole story on a first date. That's excruciating. Don't you do it, either. Remember: Ask them questions about what they do on a typical day. What were they like as a kid? Quiet? Annoying? Outgoing? A troublemaker? Information about how they acted as a kid is valuable, as they probably still retain the same main values now as they did then. I'm not talking about when they were 5-year-olds. I'm talking about 9-or-10-year-olds and older.

It really helps to have a funny or amazing short story of your own to tell them on your first date. Maybe something about you during your childhood that was cute or funny. It will help keep things lighthearted and fun, and it might remind him of a fun story to share with you. Sharing builds trust in one another, but please, again, don't over-share. He's not a sounding board for you or you for him!

Also, please don't bring your cell phone on a date with you unless it's turned off or in your purse, and please don't put it on the table. There is truly nothing worse than being at a first meet with a cell phone between you. Someone else you or he has dated previously might be sending "Hi, baby" messages. A cell phone may start ringing during your conversation. It just stops the momentum of your conversation.

There is no good reason for a cell phone to be present. Just don't do it!

Also, while on your date, if your meet is looking at his phone or constantly texting on his phone, get up and leave. No matter what story he gives you about how important a message is, *nobody* is that important, and a guy who does this is never good-looking enough to insult you like that. Leave. Say nothing. Just leave. He is an arrogant jerk who already doesn't respect you or your time. Go—move on from this guy quicker than a New York minute. You deserve better than that!

By the way, you may have heard of serial daters. These are the people—men or women—who just want to go out with as many people as they can. They are not looking for love or the right person—just having fun in the online playground. A serial dater can be what I call a "Captain Crunch," but sometimes, when you least expect it, you might meet a "Lucky Charm"! Just some corny humor there!

Remember, prepare for the encounters. You set the stage! Just be sure you give as good as you get on a date. Work hard to give your date the attention and fun he deserves. After all, he's picking up the check (yes, always on a first, second, or third date) *not to mention giving you his time!* After that, if you see him more than a few times, he will be thrilled with a home-cooked meal. If you can respect a person's time and finances, you will become successful at dating!

Feel the moment. Seize the rest. Make it happen!

CHAPTER FIFTEEN

Making the Meet Happen

*m*any guys like to text. It is fine to set up a meeting by texting. Most times, it is better. But don't get into texting a lot before you meet. Some cute texts are great to get, but don't invest yourself into back-and-forth texting before you meet. You will most likely end up being disappointed or saying something that turns him off—or he you. As I'm sure you know, texts don't really convey the emotion or playfulness of what's being said. Also, it takes away some of the excitement of the meet.

It is so important to meet face to face before you start thinking about him. If he is nothing like you built him up to be, you will get disheartened about dating after meeting him, causing you to be down on the dating pool. You will disconnect yourself from the process. Then, after a month or so, you'll pick it up again. But by then, you've lost your momentum, and it's like you're starting all over again, which is not good for you.

Which brings me to another matter. If someone emails you on Thursday for a Friday meet, that's OK if you don't have another date. Try to have your schedule open, and don't plan definite girlfriend time every week on a Friday. If you get an email on Saturday morning to meet that evening for a drink, that's a red flag, but it's still your call. Personally, I've turned them down even if I was open that evening. I figure that, if they really are interested, they could have contacted me sooner. I don't need to be any guy's second or third choice for the evening because they're bored and want company.

However, I will tell them, "I already have plans, but how about setting something up for early next week?" Then give them an option of times for two different days: "How about Monday evening for a drink at the wine bar?" (or any other restaurant/bar of your choice) or "I'm also available Wednesday morning for coffee." This way, you're not shutting them down when they want to meet with you. You're just letting them know they will be lucky to get a chance to meet you.

That's not arrogant—it just keeps your self-esteem at a good level and lets them know your value. Don't make it too easy for them, but don't make it so hard for them to meet you that they give up. Again, it's really about your comfort zone. If you, too, are bored and just want to get out, then meet them that evening.

Really, late-afternoon Sunday or Monday-evening meets are best for a first meet. If your meets are on Sunday through Wednesdays, you just may have your pick of who you want to be with on the following Friday- or Saturday-night date!

Note this: If a guy is really into seeing you again after a first meet, he will want to cement a Saturday-evening date with you early on. That's why I recommend meets in the early part of the week. They lead to weekend second dates unless the guy is playing around or already has a girlfriend. Beware of the guy who is always busy on a Friday or Saturday night but can always take you out during the week. Some guys are just on a site to look at the gals. In *most* cases, I have found out that he either had a girlfriend or wife he was playing around on. He may be with them but is still hunting for someone else he finds more exciting to be with. Unfortunately, ladies, not all men are honorable.

Beware of the guy who has his profiles hidden. Hidden profiles usually tell you he has a girlfriend or wife and is just looking at pictures. It's kind of like soft porn. They are playing. They may even meet you for breakfast or lunch—or even a drink—but it will end early.

If a guy takes you out a few times, say, a Tuesday one week, a Saturday another week, and a Friday yet a different week, he is most likely seeing a couple of other girls. You won't know it, but 99% of the time, he's playing the Internet field.

And, let's face it: If you're not sure he's your boyfriend, then, trust me: He's not. If he's really into you, there will be no guessing. Also, some guys and girls will playdate 2–3 different people at a time. If you are having sex with him and he has stories about why he can't make it every weekend, give yourself a reality check before you get any further involved with him. I'm just saying all is fair in the online dating game. You could be playing the field yourself, just as he is. But, then you probably wouldn't be falling in love with him. You will know if a guy is into you after he meets you, if he is calling you a couple of times a week, texting and asking you out in the early part of the week for a Friday or Saturday night. He is taking no chances that someone will beat him to the punch.

You should meet as many people as possible in a week. Set a goal for how many men per week. I, myself, have set up meets in one morning in the same place an hour or so apart. It can be a bit stressful, but you should attempt a coffee meet for mornings, afternoons, and on the weekends. Your goal should be to set up at least 3–4 first meets in a week: Monday through Thursday evenings, or a Saturday or Sunday morning. For a second meet, it should be a Friday or Saturday night, with one of the same guys you met earlier in the week.

Do Not . . .

Again, do not let your first meet extend for more than two hours in the evening, no matter how good or bad a time you're having. If it's in the morning or afternoon, an hour—tops! Leave something for a second date so you'll get to know if you like the person enough to go for a third.

And vice versa. Third Dates are key! They are the romance dates! And, by the way, my belief is that, if you want to have sex with a date, it won't matter if it's on the first date, third date, or tenth date. If he respects and likes you, it won't be an issue later on in your relationship, if it grows to that. Sometimes you may worry that if you sleep together, he'll think you're easy. It has nothing to do with that. If you are both into each other, there are no rules. You may want to kiss him in the first 10 minutes, or he you. That's what's called strong physical attraction! Women worry too much that if they "give it up," the man will not see them again. If he is into you. it won't matter. However, if he is into three other gals, you'll know it. Beware of the guy who says to you, "You're an awesome girl" or something like that. I'll bet you he is sleeping with others! I say the rule is "There are no rules." Follow your gut, and if you're wrong, so what? Chalk it up to experience! Move on, and forget it. Life is too short to beat yourself up over any guy. Don't let people judge you. Be your own person, and own what you do in life!

What to Say on a First Meet and What Not to Say

*L*isten to what your meet tells you. Believe it or not, he will divulge what is important to him within the first five or ten minutes. A first meet I had talked non-stop about his daughter and son-in-law for the first thirty minutes. Seriously, after that amount of time, I finally got a word in, and it was, "Thanks for the glass of champagne. It was good to meet you, but I don't think we're a match," and I got up to go. He was confused—and rightfully so. He didn't know what he had done. What he did was use me as a sounding board to talk about his daughter and son-in-law. Now it would have been OK to mention them for a minute or so, but 30 minutes straight? When he said, "How could you know that we're not a match after just thirty minutes?" I wanted to say, "I knew after five minutes!" But he wouldn't have gotten it, so I just said, "Because I know myself."

Just listen, and take it in. Does he talk about family, hobbies, match dates? Is he obsessed with talking about his grandkids? Does he go on and on? Forthright talk is great, but it needs to be about things he is interested in and wants to get across to you—and only in small, 5-minute vignettes. The same goes for you. Think about what you say. Do you drone on and on about the same thing? He's not a girlfriend who will listen to you do that, nod her head, and agree with you. Do you divulge just a bit too much information about yourself right away?

Then there's the other side. If he doesn't divulge a lot of info, it tells you he plays his cards close to his chest or he doesn't feel the need to tell you about his personal life. Respect that.

Ask him questions that give you an insight into his character.

Don't ask, "What do you do for fun?" That question is so open-ended that it won't tell you much, and it is hard for anyone to answer.

Instead ask him, "What's a typical day like for you?"

"What time of day is your favorite?"

"What's a favorite childhood memory?" If you can get a glimpse into his childhood, often, that will give you a good idea of the type of person he is now. If he had a terrible childhood, he may have a miserable adulthood. If he doesn't mention family, it's because he may have issues with them, or they with him.

No friends to speak of? There may be problems in his ability to get along with people. You can learn a lot about a person if you know what he did or felt as a child. If he tells you about treacherous deeds as a child, you might assume that treachery followed him into adulthood.

Look for argumentative behavior, if he speaks negatively about his life, family, or friends. Decide what you can accept and what you can't. If he talks only about himself and doesn't ask any questions about you, it can be a sign he is self-absorbed, maybe ego driven, or he just isn't "into you." Older men will often brag about privileged jobs they have had, how they made money in previous years, or how he used to live a great lifestyle and traveled everywhere. The question is not what they used to do or have done. Concentrate on what they do or have *now*.

However, never ask about their income. It is a rude question, and you'll come off as a gold digger. You should be able to figure out how they sustain themselves today, not years ago.

I have had guys ask me on a first meet, "So, how old are you?" I tell them, "It's on my profile." But polite men don't ask a woman's age, now, do they? I had one guy really push me on the age subject. He was questioning what I was doing in certain years. "How old are your kids?" By the way, my kids actually kept getting younger over the years, because I kept looking younger than my age. I really don't want to age gracefully. Be thankful for all that's available to us in cosmetics!

But this guy would not let up and kept trying to add the years up and so on. Of course, he was also the guy who brought 15 vitamins with him to our drink/dinner meet and was continually swallowing them during our conversation. Anyway, I felt there was no need for him to press the age subject, and I just smiled and stopped answering his questions. He couldn't let it go (red flag). He said, "Most women lie about their age on these dating sites." I finally said to him, "Show me your bank accounts, and I'll show you my birth certificate." End of the age subject!

But, it got worse. He complained about the wait for the food. It finally arrived, and, after I had eaten only half of my dinner and was finished, he eyed my food and asked me if I was going to take the rest home with me. I said, "No." He said, "Do you mind if I take it?" Of course, I said "No. You go right ahead." Now, this guy was a wealthy stockbroker. While I have told you that you don't pay for your food on a date—and rightfully so—I wanted out of there, pronto. So, I took out my credit card and said to him, "I'll split the check." He said to me, "You don't know how much you just really scored points with me." OMG! Did I care? Like I would ever see him again! This was one of the first meets I ever had, in my early online dating years. I tell you this because you will meet all kinds of guys out there. It does, however, keep online dating very interesting. Just some food for thought.

Don't Ask, Don't Tell

First meets are not a place to ask about previous relationships. You will find that many men will want to tell you everything about their relationships right away. I don't know why. It's like they feel they have to vomit everything out right away, so you know all about them quickly. Listen, but steer them away from that area, and ask questions about the last movie he saw, book he read, etc. You don't need to tell him your relationship stories on a first date. Remember this is just a meet-and-greet. Your first meet should give you insight into his mannerisms. Do you like his tone of voice? His diction? The way he holds himself? Does he treat you with respect right away? Does he act like a gentleman? Does he offer to get you a coffee or drink right away? Are you and he attracted to one another? Are there sparks? Can you see yourself giving him a kiss as he is leaning toward you to talk and is centered on you and not distracted by others around you? Do you both make good eye contact? If you don't have positive feelings after 30 minutes, you won't have them after 30 days. Move on. Give him no more than one hour of time, and thank him for the drink and for coming out to meet you. If he seems more into you, he may not want to end it. Tell him you have an early day tomorrow or another appointment to go to. You do not have to expand on your plans. You do not have to make up a lie about where you're going. You just need to leave.

I have been truthful with a few guys right away and told them I didn't think we were a match. I didn't feel any chemistry. Nothing you can do about that, right? They sometimes want to know if there's something wrong with them, as they have not been having any luck on their first meets. If you see why—he has nose hair so long you could braid it, or he didn't stop talking about himself—you can help the guy out. I have told guys what turned me off about them if I felt it would really help them on future dates. Seriously, these guys thanked me. People can't see themselves sometimes, and, many times, no one is going to tell them that they come across as too needy.

Help a guy out if you can, even though he may not be for you. You might help him to find someone who is right for him.

So, consider the guy who shows up on a first meet with flowers, buys you lots of drinks and dinner, and all the while, his comments seem to be full of sexual innuendoes. He is setting you up to have sex with him. If not for the first meet, he is setting you up for the second one. If you're out to have fun, go for it. If not, move on.

CHAPTER SEVENTEEN

The Pickup Option
Should I let them pick me up at my place?

i always get asked this question regarding being picked up at your home or workplace. Do I always meet my first date somewhere like a coffee shop, bar, park, etc.? If you both have decided to go out for dinner and feel confident that you know enough about him, there is no reason why he can't pick you up—especially if you've already had a lengthy phone conversation. You have to go with your gut on this. The stories about guys abducting women from online dating at our age are fairy tales. I mean, really: Most of the online men older than 50 are not looking to steal us or abduct us for the slave market. We are not some hot gal in her twenties. We're too expensive and set in our ways, and we would probably be such a pain in their ass that they would beg to give us back!

But back to the question. If a date offers to pick you up, I say, "Go for it." As a matter of fact, if you want to be picked up so you don't have worry about drinking and driving or a DUI, ask him if he'd like to pick you up. You can offer to meet him outside of where you live. Tell him to text you when he's 5 minutes away, as you don't want to keep him waiting. He may say, "No, I'll come to get you at your door." Consider him a gentleman or just nosy to see your place. More likely, he's hoping to get some romance in at the end of the evening with you.

Men love to pick up their dates at our age, especially first dates. It's what they grew up doing, only they won't need to meet your parents—unless you live with them! It seems like a real date to them, and it gives them an excuse to wash their car. If they are going to take you to dinner, I think they deserve to "orchestrate the dinner." If they ask you where you want to eat, the better. But be fair: Pick a place you're comfortable in but is not overly expensive. I'm not saying Olive Garden, but a nice restaurant that's reasonable and romantic. If they don't ask you and surprise you, that's good. Lucky girl! But if you think it's an sub-par restaurant, hopefully you'll enjoy the company, if not the food.

That reminds me of one of my first dates when I let the gentleman pick me up. He said that we were going to one of his favorite Italian restaurants and that he knew the owner really well. It was on Sunset Blvd. Being new to the Southern California area, I had never eaten there. It was lovely, we had an outdoor table, he introduced me to the owner, knew our waiter, etc. Wonderful, fun meal, great conversation, super guy.

The next night, I had a different date. He picked me up and said he was going to take me to one of his favorite restaurants! He knew the owner and said the food was delicious. Yes, you guessed it. With all the restaurants in Southern California near my apartment, he takes me to the same restaurant! I couldn't believe it! He introduces me to the owner, who, by the way, made like it was the first time he had ever met me. He gave us a table, and it was right next to the one I had sat at the night before. To top it all off, we had the same waiter who, professional that he was, acted like he had never seen me before. I just smiled and carried on. I did order a different dish. Then I started thinking, on the off chance, that maybe these two guys knew each other, but that was just overthinking it! I came to the conclusion that they both just had good taste in very romantic Italian restaurants. And they both knew that I previously owned an Italian restaurant! So chalk it up to coincidence and an effort to please their date!

Back to the picking up at your place. After dinner or whatever event, the evening draws to a close, and he's walking you to your door. It is up to you to invite him in for an after-dinner drink or coffee if you really are having a great time. It's early, and you just don't want the evening to end. (Hopefully, if you do that, you thought about your place being neat and tidy before you left.) You call the shots here. Again, the decision is yours alone. You either thank him for a fun evening when you reach your door (insert key), he gives you a hug or a kiss and says goodnight. Or you invite him to come in. If you do invite him in, try to arrange it so he's sitting across from—not next to—you. Why, you ask? This way, you and he get to look at each other, really look into each other's eyes. It's the best way to see if there's real attraction with each other. Let the excitement mount; make him want to see you again very soon. Let the conversation flow. Of course, in doing that, you have to know when you want him to leave. No need to hint at it. Don't use the yawn and "I have to get up early in the morning." Just be straight with him. Say, "This has been such a fun evening, but it's time to say goodnight." If he's not willing to get up, you should get up, walk to the door, and open it with a "Thanks for a super great time!" He will leave. Smile a huge smile upon his exit, and then close the door.

That's it! Be firm, but sweet and simple. Just because you let him linger for a while at your place, it does not have to amount to "Let's jump in bed."

If you feel more comfortable meeting him at a restaurant, bar, whatever—that's great, too. I'm just trying to tell you not to get stuck on being afraid of having a date coming to get you. As I said before, I have met more than 500 men in eleven years. A very good number of these dates have picked me up at my residence. I have never had an issue, and I have never heard of an issue from other gals who meet and date online. By the way, I suggest this if you are going somewhere within a 10–15 mile radius of where you live.

And some good information comes out of being picked up by your date. This is a great way to judge his mannerisms, his confidence, his driving habits. Does he maneuver the car well while having a conversation with you? If he isn't sure of the place you two are going to, it allows you to be a good navigator and help him get there. Does he let you do this or tell you, "I've got it."? That can be a good determination for how you'll work together in a situation. Is it easy or stressful?

Sometimes, you just need to take a risk when you're dating. Just listen to yourself, and go with your gut. After all, that's how you move forward into feeling confident in the dating world.

CHAPTER EIGHTEEN

After the First Date

How to Have the Next One or How to Say "Goodbye"

So, you've had your first meeting with him. Let's say it was drinks and appetizers in the evening. You're excited about him—good vibrations, lots of laughs, hugged each other maybe, hopefully had a kiss when saying goodbye. Remember Cher's song? "It's in his kiss!" Most times, it is.

So, now you are both on your way home, "high on the meet," maybe still wanting to stay connected to each other. Here's where you can go wrong.

Do not text him right after the meet. If he sends you a text, give yourself at least 30–60 minutes before you respond. If he is texting right after the date, it should be to set up the next date and not because he's bored and wants someone to talk to or have telephone sex with you because he's excited about you. Oh yeah, they do that. They're men. Look: There is no right or wrong answer here or judgment about how you should handle this. Just make sure you are not taken advantage of because of his lust. Play this game only because you also want to play—not because you think he'll like you better.

Once you have made the next date with him, it is okay to text once in a while until your second date. Do not text each other multiple times a day. It is too soon, and he and you will get bored before you even get to the point of a second date. Anticipation is a very important factor in seeing each other again. Don't dilute it with hours of phone calls or texts. Remember, face to face will tell you if he and you are feeling a sufficient amount of chemistry to move on to another date. The real issue should be: Does he have the attributes you are looking for in a mate—one with whom you see a future? Nothing is written in stone, but the stronger you feel about him and where you two are headed, the better the chance he will be the right guy for you.

But, let's say he's not the right guy for you after the meet—and you know it!

Rules of Disengagement

OK, so you have no interest in him, he's not what you're looking for, or there was no chemistry. You don't want to hear from him again. How do you handle that? You'll need to email him the next day after your first meet. I call this "making the cut." You should email a "thank you" note within 24 hours, especially if he had paid for drinks, lunch, or dinner. It is courteous, respectful, and the right thing to do. It's what classy women do.

A short note saying, "It was great meeting you. Thanks for drinks and eats" (or dinner) would be appropriate. Be sure to include the "thank you" for coffee, drinks, or appetizer, dinner—I assume you would have had one of these during your meet with him. And thank him for picking up the check for you—and he should have done that!

If you liked him and want to see him again, you should add, "I had a lot of fun, and I'm looking forward to getting together again with you very soon!"

If you don't want to see him again, then you need to add a "Goodbye" to the email. The email should be kind but definite in your intention to not see him again. You should email him after your meet. Best to do this by the morning after your evening date or within one day of your coffee meet.

The sooner you do it, the better.

Examples of "Cut" emails:

Hi _____ . Thank you so very much for the coffee and interesting conversation. I enjoyed learning about you. Unfortunately, I feel we're not a match for each other. Good luck to you in your search! Sincerely, _____ (your first name).

Dear _____: It was fun spending time with you and exchanging stories and ideas! While you are a great guy, I don't believe the two of us are a life match, and that's what I'm looking for. Good luck in your search!

Best, _____ (your first name)

No one likes to write what I call "cut' emails—*or* receive them—and you will receive them. But, keep in mind that it is necessary to move on and concentrate on the next meet. You need to look at dating as you would a job search. It's the same technique, and the purpose is to get the interview, find out what it's all about, and decide if it fits into your needs or goals.

It may seem cold, but it is way better than to ignore his texts or phone calls. It's also useless to go on talking to or dating someone who is not what you really are looking for.

Please don't just say you're busy if he calls or texts you to go out again or seems really interested in you. Don't be a coward. Let him know how you feel, so he, too, can move on.

If you get a "Thanks, but no thanks" email from a guy, be gracious no matter what you thought. You do not need to spend time wondering what he did or didn't like about you or if you did something wrong. You didn't!

It just didn't click for him, and there may be many reasons. Maybe he's doing a lot of online first meets and is pursuing other interests. Maybe he's still in love with someone else and is dating to fall out of love with that person. Maybe he just didn't feel it with you. It happens to all of us.

Whatever. Don't waste your time on someone who isn't connecting with you.

If he is a classy-enough person to contact you with his "cut" email, write him back a simple line. "I totally understand. Good luck in your search!" If the guy has any integrity, he will write a "not a match" email instead of just not emailing or calling you and leave you dangling, wondering if you'll ever hear from him again.

Guys who are active and dating a couple of meets a week usually wait to see where things go with each of their meets—keep the fish swimming in the pond, so to speak. So, you may hear nothing for a week, two, or three weeks, and, then, out of the blue, you get an email from them. Maybe their original-choice meet didn't work out, so they go on to the next. This happens all the time. And it will and should happen with you, too, if you are making the effort to meet as many profiles as you can. Note: If you are first on their list and have piqued their interest, you will be hearing from them within a few days of your first meet. You will be doing the same with your choice meets also.

If, after 2–3 dates, *you* decide if it's not going to work, you can use the telephone to say goodbye. Do not email or text or just ignore his phone calls. You should call him. Give it to him straight. If you have ever been let go from a company after just a few weeks, remember what they said to you: "We appreciate your time, but we don't think it's a good fit for either of us." Yes, you are fired. So, how are you going to fire him? With a short-but-sweet statement like this: "I enjoyed going to the places we went together. I had a great time, and I thank you for those times, but I just don't feel we are relationship material for the future."

Try to do this on a Sunday or Monday, when he can process what he may have thought was amazing about the two of you being together, and it finally sinks in that you didn't feel the same as he may have. It will give him time to jump back in the online dating game after a day or two and start searching for another weekend date. Remember: The best way to get over someone is to get on with (or under) someone else!

If you decide to say, "Goodbye" after 4–5 dates, *you* need to pull up those big-girl pants and do it in person. I'm talking eye-to-eye breakup. What do you say? How do you say it? Be straight and kind, but firm. Something like:

"I'm just not feeling what I need to feel for you to move on with this relationship. I can't change or force a feeling that I thought might have been there but is not there any longer."

It's true: You can't *make* yourself feel love for someone. At this point in life, you should both realize you either feel it, or you don't. Maybe love was mentioned by you? You need to just tell him that you've lost that loving feeling. You don't need to go into why or when, even if he has done certain things to turn you off. Unless you are feeling magnanimous, tell him what those things were. Maybe it can help him with his next relationship—and yours, too. Seriously, try to give something back to people whose paths you cross in the dating world. It's hard for everyone out there, and everyone needs to play nice. Maybe you'll give him some food for thought for the next gal.

But, what if he was a really good date? You see each other a few times, start having a lot of fun, but you know it's just for fun, not a relationship. Maybe there's a huge age difference or you're both in the wrong place to have an ongoing future relationship. So, you go out and have fun, and you know what it is—just fun and games. Good for you! Well, enjoy it, but be careful what you share about him with your grown-up kids (if you have them), Especially, if, like my kids, they are always watchful of what they sometimes refer to as "their teenage mom." There are a few good stories about my online dating and things that gave my kids some concern. But, this one takes the cake: I was, at the time (a young 56), living in Beverly Hills, dating a much younger man, a doctor. We had such fun together, but we both knew it what it was: A friendship and a lot of sexually charged fun. He would get off at the hospital at around 11:00 PM and would then pick me up, and we'd go out to some very fun, exclusive restaurants or dance clubs. We'd drink expensive champagne and kick our heels up! Exciting, happy fun! I mean, who's not up for that? My kids knew about my online dating and were, at times, protective of me. I told them about him and how we'd go out late or sometimes meet for lunch.

My kids did not believe he was a doctor. They briefly met him one time. He didn't look like a typical doctor to them. He was tall, handsome, and, well, he was a lot younger than me. Now, I knew he was a doctor, and I also knew he was a player, but it didn't bother me at the time, because I was playing then, too. He would come and pick me up in different, beautiful, expensive cars all the time. I'd say, Where do you get all these great cars?" He'd say, "My car-dealer friend lets me take a different car out of his dealership—basically, whenever I want."

Well, my kids, who think they are a cross of Nancy Drew and the Hardy Boys, decided to play detective. And the different car every week didn't sound right to them. So my daughter calls me up at 11:00 PM and says, "What are you doing, mom?" I'd say, "Michael is here. We're in tonight, having tacos and tequila!" She'd say, "Is he there right now?" and I'd say 'Yes'." And there it went: They have a good friend who is a police officer, and they involve him in this caper. So, my son-in-law drives to my apartment and then drives up and down the block and jots down license-plate numbers of possible "suspects" car types that are parked on my street at that moment. Their good friend checks out these car plates, and bingo! "The Caper Kids" figure out what's going on.

The next day, they very seriously ask me to come over because they need to talk to me. When I get there, they proceed to tell me that my "Michael boy" is no doctor. Really? "Yes," they say (wait for it), "he's a limousine driver!"

Now, I am a pretty savvy woman and have a good sense about people and a good sense of humor (after all, I'm a New York girl). I say, "You guys are crazy!" I mean I am laughing so hard, there are tears rolling down my face. "No," they say, "we checked all the cars out, and the only one that could be his is registered to a limousine company." What could I do? Trying not to laugh, I call this "limousine driver/doctor friend" and tell him the story while I'm still at my kids' apartment building. He happens to be off work. He tells me to stay right there—he'll be right over. 15 minutes later, he knocks on the door and shows my very embarrassed children a framed certificate of his medical degree. He is laughing as hard as I am! He then tells them that he had to park three blocks away the evening of "the investigation." A month or so after this incident, the four of us decided we would all ride together to see a concert. He came to pick us up—in a limo! No, he wasn't driving. But he did borrow the limo driver's cap and had it on his head when he knocked at the door! Now, that was funny, and that's a guy with great sense of humor!

So, be forewarned: If you have older children watching out for you, and they sometimes use your dating escapades as entertainment for themselves, you can expect a few surprises from them!

CHAPTER NINETEEN

Date, Date, Date, and Then Date Again

*t*his is why I tell you to connect with as many people as possible online. You won't care too much about one person not calling you if you have others to pursue or they are pursuing you!

Keep searching!

There will be times you will wonder if you should go out and have another date with someone who, after the first date, didn't ring your chimes. You may be indecisive and will make excuses for him or yourself about the date—acceptable reasons why you think maybe you need to see him again. Just to be sure.

Honestly, if the first date didn't thrill you or was mediocre, don't—and I *mean* "don't"—go on a second date. 98% of the time, you will just feel the same way as you did the first time you were together—heck, maybe even worse. But if you are really on the fence about him, by all means, go ahead. You will find that your tendency is to "give it another chance." However, do not keep going out with someone just because he asks you out and you have nothing else going on. Spend your effort on someone you haven't met yet instead of someone who was just "alright."

There will be the men who don't feel it for you but will lead you on to let you think they do. Some guys like to keep a playing field of ladies around for many reasons. It could be his ego, someone to eat dinner with, or just someone to have sex with. Could be all of the above. Maybe they really don't want a girlfriend or commitment. Just be aware and true to yourself about your relationship with him. If you're not sure, ask him straight out! If you don't want to be part of the playing field, tell him. If he really is interested, he will drop the others and see where things go with you.

If, on a first date, guys ask you things like, "Would you ever get married again?" it can mean he's really wanting to settle down—or that he's baiting you. Men know that most women do want to have the commitment of marriage, and if they are looking to get with you physically—and, God knows, they all do—then they are playing with you.

You have to know the rules!

Men want sex. Women want security. End of story!

Why he doesn't call when he said he'd be in touch

He isn't too busy. He hasn't lost your number. He hasn't been in an accident. His dog didn't die. There wasn't a death in his family. He isn't "loaded down with work." He doesn't have too many responsibilities (kids, mother, etc). He just doesn't want to. As the line goes, "He's just not that into you."

Sorry . . . Don't shoot the messenger . . .

Why he calls only once in a while or sends you a short text every day

He is keeping you in his pond of fishes. He is dating other women. He does not want a girlfriend; he does not want a commitment. He does not want to meet "the one." He is playing and wants nothing more than someone to give him attention when he feels the need to get it. Whether it's someone to go places with or someone to have sex with, he wants your time on his schedule. That's OK if you just want to be an escort . . . but, **do not fall in love with this guy. He will break your heart. No matter how much you don't think he knows that you're crazy about him, trust me: He knows.**

If he's a decent guy, he will not keep dating you and leading you on. It isn't anything you said or did wrong. It's him, not you. So what do you do?

Move on, move on, move on.

Do not think he will come around to really like you in time. He won't like you any more on the second or third date than he did on the first. Don't waste your time! Enough said!

CHAPTER TWENTY

Keep a Spreadsheet on Your Dates

*Y*es, like an Excel spreadsheet of some kind, nothing fancy. If you are doing what you should be doing about dating—meaning, dating a few different men each week—you will need to do this.

When you are putting together a lot of first meets, you should keep a log on them so you can keep it straight. The log should show who you're meeting and the key points about them in case they call you. You'll have it handy to know who you're really talking to and what you should be talking about.

It should look something like this:

Date/Time/Place/His Site Name/His Real Name/City/Key Points/Site Met

3/15 6 PM, Daily Grill, drinks, "RUNNERFORYOU," aka-TOM, Westlake, attorney, 3 kids, scuba, widow, *Match.com* site

3/16 10 AM, Starbucks, coffee, "LUV2SKI," aka BOB, West LA, accountant, dog is 'Spot,' hiking, sushi, martini, divorced, *OurTime.com* site

3/16 7 PM, Lure's, dinner, "GOLFER65," aka LARRY, Ventura, Wine Salesman, golfer, 2 children, divorced, *Match.com* site

3/18 5 PM, Mastro, drinks, "LOOKING4U," aka MARK, Beverley Hills, sports broadcaster, basketball season pass, flies his own plane, never married, millionaire, *Match.com* site

Otherwise you will be downloading profiles and getting them mixed up. When that happens—and it will—you will embarrass yourself when you bring up their golf game and they don't golf or children he doesn't have.

They will not feel "special," and, possibly that will blow it for you, because they think they are just one of your many guys. They are, but you don't need to tell them that. They might ask you how you are finding the site. Just be positive and tell them, "It's been fun, and I've met some very nice, interesting people."

Do not tell your meets how many meets you have had or didn't have in a week, month, ever. Don't ever talk about other dates. Certainly, you should print out his profile and take it with you when you go to meet him. Read it before you go in to meet him. Leave it in the car. But keep his profile turned over on the seat next to you in case he walks you to your car, which, if he's any kind of gentleman, he will do.

OK—*you've met him at the destination*

Sometimes, they will want to tell you about their "horror dates" if they are not doing well on the site or if they are trying to get a conversation going with you. Maybe they have been disenchanted with the gals who have cancelled their meet five minutes before, or who didn't even show up, or who didn't look like their photos at all, etc. They are wondering if they are doing something wrong and are trying to get you to give them information; they may assume you have to justify their experiences. Everyone will have a disappointing date once in a while. Do not share dating "horror stories." Best to say, "Yes, online dating has its ups and downs and can be challenging." Because once you start sharing stories, it will take any romance that you might have had started with him out of the equation. You'll be just another story for his catalog. Anyhow, neither of you should be talking about other people you have met on the site. The purpose of the meet is to share stories and opinions about each other. Bringing other people into the conversation will dilute that. Keep it about the two of you. Your likes, books, travel, fun stuff. Keep the conversation simple, and keep it positive and fun. Tell him a joke if you have to. He is not there as your sounding board about your rotten friend or bad luck, and neither are you there for his terrible boss or jerk of a coworker. This is all about fun, laughing, and light conversation.

Your job is to keep everyone straight. Remember who you're meeting and what they are about. Also, I would give them a star rating at the end of the date on the spreadsheet. So, if you really liked someone, they were a good date, and you wanted to see them again, I would put (4)★★★★ by their name. If I didn't want to see them again and send them a cut email, I would put (1)★. If you think it can't get confusing, it sure can. I once had four dates in the week, and their names all happened to be "Mark." That was a strange coincidence, but it did happen and it's just how some things go. So you need to have a system to keep your wits about you and keep each person special. Remember to put a mark on Mark.

CHAPTER TWENTY-ONE

What Should Be a Turnoff on a First Meet

(or maybe any meet)

1. He's late—more than 5 minutes unless he texted or called and even if he did, If he's not there in 20 minutes from the call, leave. He would have been on time if you were important. After all, you spent time on makeup and clothes, and you're on time. Chalk it up.

2. He's not attentive. He's looking around, maybe eyeing the other gals in the place. BTW, if he's eyeing the other guys in the place, re-think this date totally!

3. He disses his ex-wife, his kids, his siblings, his co-workers. He's an unhappy, judgmental individual. Run.

4. He is way ahead of you on drinks. His 4 to your 1.

5. He doesn't offer to get food of any type. If you're having drinks, he should offer to get an appetizer or something, even if you don't want one. Especially

if he looks at the bar menu and still doesn't ask you, or if the waiter asks you both, and he answers "No" for you, too.

6. He talks to other women around you, sitting at the bar, etc. Even if he knows them, it should just be to say hello or a few words to acknowledge them. He should be focused on you.

7. He keeps his cell phone on the bar. He looks at it from time to time—even answers text messages while you're sitting next to him. You are outta there! Go!

8. He is rude to the help or doesn't acknowledge them. Or, he is overly chatty with the help. Again, the focus should be on you.

9. He casually asks if you've had work done—i.e., plastic surgery.

10. He asks you if you want to split the check. You can say "Yes" if you want but with the disclaimer to him that he should take a photo of you—because he's never going to see you again! The man picks up the check—always.

11. He doesn't ask many questions about you. He talks a lot about himself but doesn't question you. He just wants to talk about himself.

12. He talks over you when you start speaking. You are cut short of your conversation or your side of the discussion.

13. He arrives with breathing apparatus or a walker. Seriously, don't think it hasn't happened

14. He says "Huh?" twenty or more times during the conversation. Unless it is extremely noisy during your meet, he has forgotten his hearing aid or doesn't want you to know he has one.

15. He talks about all the other beautiful women he's dated.

16. He asks what your real age is. Screw him—and I don't mean literally.

17. He asks if you're wearing panties or a bra. With a smile on his face. Like he's cute. He's not.

18. He tells you that you have nice breasts, ass, or legs. That's OK, by the way, on a third date. OK—maybe second, but not first.

19. He asks how many men you've been sexually active with. Ask him how many times he's jerked off—this month.

20. He asks about your income—in any way, shape, or form.

21. He sends you a text with a picture of his private parts within 15 minutes after your date ends. You can tell him you had to enlarge the photo 100% just to see it.

CHAPTER TWENTY-TWO

The Second Date

*i*f you've gotten through the first meet/date and you are excited for the second—*great!* He may ask you at the end of the first date when he can see you again. Ask him if you can get back to him later as you don't have your schedule for the week with you. A little mystery is always in order. Also, if you don't like him enough for a second date, you will need to send him the cut email.

But, the second date happens, and he arrives. He picks you up at your house or a location outside it. This is a very important date, because you need to really focus on whether he has what you're looking for. It's easier to do the cut after a first or second date. The third is really a hard one because there's an investment, mentally and physically, on his and your part.

The second date is going to show you different aspects of him. Don't go to a movie if you can help it. That wastes valuable, informative talking time. Dinner in a relatively quiet place is a good choice or an event at a fair while you're walking around. Any place that you two will seem comfortable enough to really discuss what's important to each other in your lives and how you both are planning to achieve it. There should be a lot of eye contact, general conversation, and a whole lot of laughter. At this point, you probably will discuss past marriages, relationships, and children, and you will learn a lot about each other on this date.

Laughter is the necessary key in a relationship. The more, the better, and it shouldn't be one-sided. You should both have a rapport going between you and give as good as you are getting. I don't care how good a "catch" he is. If you are not making each other laugh, you will be bored by the fifth date.

At our age, we need to be very aware of what makes us happy. Let's face it, we don't have the luxury to fool around for a few months and wonder if it's going to go somewhere.

If you have to wonder where you are with him in a relationship, you are kidding yourself. If it's seriously the "right one" for both of you, you will know this and at some point, both of you will be talking about what you envision your future to look like. After all, maybe you have a good 25 years left in life. Some more, some less, depending on your age. But it's not like when you were thirty, forty, or even fifty. You are going into your golden years, and if you don't want to be in them alone, you need to be diligent about finding "the right one" at this point. Don't waste your efforts in dating. It takes a lot of work, so work smart.

I had a relationship with a gentleman who had it all going for him: Looks, money, (some bad jokes, but still). He was charming when you met him and gave a good impression.

But, I started to see some red flags after the first five weeks. On one occasion, I met his daughter, a very pretty 17-year-old girl. We picked her up to take her to dinner. I was appalled at how he spoke to her. He treated her with such disrespect and unkindness. He spoke to her as if she were worthless. He was so controlling in his conversation, and I felt the meanness come out of him. She stayed quiet while he spoke and answered him only when he demanded an answer. It was so uncomfortable, and I felt disdain for him and pity for her.

During dinner, he left the table to take a phone call, and I said to her, "Is this common in his treatment of you?" She tearfully said, "Yes." She was living with her mother, his Asian ex-wife, for whom he paid all the bills. This young girl was getting ready to go to college. His control of their money kept her and her mother in his control. It was sad. I had noticed previously his control on other issues when he was with me, but I had no idea to what extent. If you see something that's off key once, more than likely you'll see it many other times. Walk away, and look beyond the golden goose, or you could end up like a slaughtered chicken.

It is common to not really know a person early on, but keep your eyes and your mind open to what could be red flags. While I saw them, I didn't heed them, and it was a waste of time that could have been devoted toward finding "Mr. Right."

Know what is important to you, and search for the right one.

CHAPTER TWENTY-THREE

The Third Date

The Future?

*i*f you gotten to a third or maybe fourth date, you've had lots of phone conversations and texting by now, and you realize you are both really excited about moving your relationship forward. Are you sexually inspired in the same fire?

You should be considering him as a possible life mate. It is a great idea to consider taking a vacation together for a few days. Sometimes that becomes a very telling tale. If you can't get along 24/7 for a few days or a week, you two most likely won't ever get along.

Now would be the time to discuss what's important to you—what you want your future to look like, what loyalty means. It is not too early to say what you expect out of a relationship. If you want marriage, you need to let him know that's the type of commitment you are looking for. Put it on the line now. Women get afraid that, if they tell a man too soon in the relationship that they are looking for that long-term commitment, the guy will bail or get scared off. It is here that you may learn that he does not really want the same things you do. That's fine. But, if he is unsure about what he wants his future to look like, and he hesitates about ever getting married again, or he says he'll never get married again, you need to reevaluate him before you fall harder for him. If he's telling you these things straight up, believe him. Don't think that, when he gets to know you, he will fall so in love with you that he will change his mind. He won't. Realize it, and realize where your life needs to go. Stay your course. Keep looking if you're not having the same thoughts.

Money is always an issue, especially with an older man. Many feel they must leave it all to their children and are actually afraid to tell their children if they don't plan to leave it to them. That's one of the reasons a man does not want to get married. They are afraid that they'll lose their savings.

I understand that, because if you're at an age where you can't work anymore, you could be in trouble.

I like the guy who is using his own, earned money to be happy in life. He is content to do whatever he wants to, because he can. But beware of the guy, who as the saying goes, "may want his cake and eat it, too." He wants a beauty by his side, showing her the good life as long as it is what he wants her to enjoy. The enjoyment is really to his liking, and the beauty is a sidecar on his motorbike, sharing the ride and maybe never getting in the driver's seat. If that goes on for too long, you'll find out that you will get from him only what he is willing to give you, not what you really need or want. Many women commit to a man for his money. But, money can be depleted. If you don't truly like a person for who he is and not for what he has, you will find yourself miserable if things change.

CHAPTER TWENTY-FOUR

Long-Distance Dating
When He's Not a Local Meet!

S o, you're surfing on your online dating site, searching for potential meets (good job!), when, *Wham!* An email pops up from a guy in another state! Maybe from a guy whose state borders yours, maybe from a state on the other side of the country. You wonder: *Does this have potential—dating someone out of state, a plane ride away?*

Everything has potential in this situation, but the chances of the relationship surviving are thin. It is hard enough to build a relationship when someone lives close to you. It's really difficult to make one work in another state. especially, when you are older or have immediate family who live nearby. Because, eventually, even if the relationship is "the one," someone will have to uproot their life and move for it to become serious. It's easier to do this in your twenties or thirties, maybe even forty. But think about it in your 50s, 60s, 70s, or even 80s. The older you are, it may be less likely that you will get a lot of out-of-state emails. But it happens. Many older gentlemen like the advantage of having one or two pen pals to write to. It gives them something to occupy their alone time—the excitement of possibly meeting their "dream girl"! They have a better chance at winning their state lottery! I have found most of the men who constantly approach women from another state are not looking to get married. Why? If a gentleman is in his 60s or older, he has a really great chance of finding enough local women around him to get involved with. After all, women live longer than men, and there are more of them available in the golden years. Long-distance dating will leave you wanting unless what you're wanting is a pen pal, too. It is difficult and expensive if you get serious about an out-of-state mate. The nightly phone calls are usually full of "Wish we were sitting next to each other, I miss you so much" especially if you have already met. If you haven't met, but have emailed, texted, Facetimed, Skyped, or however you've been communicating, you will eventually meet. In my experience, most of these meetings will result in disappointment, no matter how much time you have spent getting to know one another. It is just not the same when you finally meet the person.

One of you and possibly both of you will not like their looks, demeanor, car, home, friends, or even how they walk.

There may be quirks you can't see from his emails or phone conversations—quirks that you don't like or think are weird—and you start to feel uncomfortable on your visit to his world or his visit to yours. All of a sudden, you just want him to go home, or you want to go home.

Also, who pays for the airfare? He should pay for the airfare. What about sleeping arrangements? If you get to the point where one of you is visiting the other, you can be sure that he expects to consummate the relationship physically, and you may or may not have considered that situation when meeting. You don't feel any attraction! It happens.

I once had a gentleman visit from New York. When I went to pick him up at the airport, the small limp he had told me about was not small at all, and for whatever reason, because I'm not one to mind disabilities, I just could not feel romantic about him—at all. I mean, I didn't even want to kiss him. He felt totally the opposite toward me. When we met, I could tell he was planning on a seriously romantic visit. Yet, during the long-distance courting, I thought it could be a real love connection! Luckily, he was staying in a hotel. He had planned to stay one week. To be cordial, I took him around to visit the local sites for two days and had dinner with him the first two nights. After that, I just didn't want to be with him. He was on his own. But, don't feel bad for him—he got over it quickly enough. He was resourceful! He went online and looked up the gals in my area and ended up taking one lady out a couple of times. It was his ticket, and I didn't blame him.

CHAPTER TWENTY-FIVE

Is There a Fairy-Tale Story?

*P*ossibly, a man would be happy to live with you and care for you as long as you two are together. If you don't get married, your relationship is considered to be a "common law" relationship—if you stick with him for seven years. But that does not give you any elder-care protection. Do not accept those terms. You need the security at your age. You don't need to worry about being "let go" at 75 years old. Say you're suddenly kicked out of his house, or maybe he passes on to the next world, and you have no place to go. Again, you could have had him put $200,000 in your own name in a savings account just for you. I mean, you need some type of stability in life. Social Security is not enough to live on these days.

If you were married to him for at least ten years, you could collect his Social Security should he die—and also his veteran pension, if he was in the service and had one, and some medical benefits. This amounts to a mere sprinkling of dollars to help you survive if you both had built nothing else together.

If you can afford to keep separate residences and you don't want a committed relationship, that's fine, if you really feel that way. Maybe you don't want to give up the fun things that you do by yourself—like the TV programs you watch. Think about that. Many women say they are happy just being alone. So, you wouldn't be looking for a mate anyway. But, if that's you, you wouldn't have bought this book, right?

Women want and need security and appreciation. Are you going to have a sexual relationship with him, wash his clothes, cook his dinner, keep house for him, and care for him when he's sick? Then, if/when he dies, it all goes to his relatives! No, you are not a "housekeeper with benefits" for him. Do not sell yourself short. If you are with someone who tells you he doesn't want to get married or commit, leave him— unless he can put a figure around $200,000 in a bank account under your name solely and add to it yearly. Then you are a vested employee. So be it, as long as you're not homeless at 75 years old. If you are in need of someone to help take care of you, you had better be sure at this point that this guy will be a stand-up guy. If not, move on. Knowledge is knowing a tomato is a fruit. Wisdom is not putting it in a fruit salad.

Which brings me to a very sad story.

Some years ago, I was in a Costco parking lot on a Saturday. I heard a racket—yelling, crying. But it wasn't a baby or teenager's racket. I went to see what was happening. An older woman, maybe in her late 60s, was yelling at a man and crying. She was saying, "You told me you were going to marry me. You told me for years that you were going to care for me, and now you tell me we're done and you want me to move out of your house? Where will I go? What will I do?" Obviously, the man had picked the time in a Costco parking lot to tell her it was over. Now, it isn't hard to figure out that he wasn't a stand-up guy. Maybe she was pushing marriage, or maybe she was just worried about her old age. Even though that man tried to calm her down, she was just beside herself.

I was compelled to watch and listen, and I was almost crying with her. I knew what was happening. I wanted to go to over to her, but the person I was with said not to get involved. He wanted to just drive away—maybe because he, too, did not want to commit to me in marriage, and he did not want to hear or see that happening to someone else. See no evil, hear no evil. But, I felt a tremendous amount of sadness, and that ignited in me a lot of reflection: Would I be her in ten years?

I moved out of that relationship a year later because I did not want to be a fatality like that poor woman. If my finances would have allowed me to move sooner, I would have. If you're in that situation, try to find a way out. I'm so glad I did, because that allowed me to go back to dating and meet the man I was supposed to be with—one who loves and adores me and honors me with himself and his life in our marriage. This man was ready, willing, and able to allay my worst fears. Burdening one of my children and living with them. They would have to try to find a place for me to live on my own that they could afford while they struggled putting their kids through college or saving for their own retirement years.

My divorces and/or poor planning for my later years should not be put on them.

The older woman without enough finances to be independent must make some kind of effort to take care of herself. It's great if you had a large divorce settlement. It's great if you can find work. It's hard to do at an older age, but say you're lucky to have skills that enable you to work on your own, not be a company employee, and still manage to make your own lifestyle a pretty good one. You won't end up eating cat food for dinner.

What happens if you get hurt you and you can't work? What will you do? How will you afford to live? Now is the time for all good women to come to their own aid!

You should do all you can to take care of yourself and to make sure you're taken care of. A real man will see taking care of a spouse and family as a responsibility and honor, not a chore from which to escape.

Find someone who knows you're not perfect but treats you as if you are!

CHAPTER TWENTY-SIX

Samples of Profiles

ITSAWOW (This Would Be Your Call Name on
   a Dating Site)
Stars in my eyes! (This would be your headline)

*e*nergy personified . . . lively, animated, genuine, and great fun to be with. I'm an adventurous soul with a happy, positive attitude. I have a sincere love of the ocean, find joy in the smell of fresh-brewed coffee, a pre-heated bed, my flick-of-a-switch fireplace, almost any music, classic movies, Monopoly, waggy dog tails, kind people, my family, and life in general.

A self-proclaimed chef who respects a perfect Martini, a well-chilled bottle of good champagne, and a decent red. I'm up for doing everything as well as doing nothing . . . Live for the moment, remember the past, and stay excited for the future. . . . and, like Disneyland. . . . I can put a smile on your face, stars in your eyes, and a "wow" on your lips . . .

Hoping you are savvy, adventurous, a leader, financially secure, somewhat sophisticated, with an easy smile. The type of man who has enjoyed building his legacy, but it does not own you. Rather, it is those experiences which have made you happy with your life's journey. That you did it your way, and it mattered, most of all . . . to you. You have an open heart and mind, and seriously yearn for the gut-wrenching feeling of being totally head over heels in love, knowing it's out there. . . . And not settling for anything less . . .

BTW: If you don't look like your picture, you're buying me drinks until you do!

———— ▪ ————

LADYOFTHEARTS (This would be your call name on a dating site—the name you're known by.)
Life is a cabaret, old friend. (This would be your headline in your profile.)

I'm kinda like a Broadway show: I sing, I dance, I act, and I play musical instruments. I have been in more than 25 theatre productions. I can play the piano and guitar, and I can sing just about any musical request. I'm lucky to know these are gifts I was given to share and enjoy with others. Now, you'll find me singing monthly at a nursing home or two-stepping on a weekly basis.

Happily, I am the mother of three wonderful children and three beautiful grandkids. As a kindergarten teacher most of my life, I've had the joy and laughter of many children who were mine only five days a week for one year of their lives.

It is humbling to know that you can touch such a young life in such a large way.

So, as another chapter of my life is ready to begin, I am looking for someone who has the same attitude, spirit, and energy as I have, along with the knowledge that passion is ageless.

If you are a confident, secure, easygoing gentleman who is looking for a good friend and companion, I'm your girl. Come join my cabaret!

———— ▪ ————

ACEOFHEARTS (This would be your call name on a dating site—the name you're known by.)
Playing with a full deck—most of the time (This would be your headline.)

I'm a card shark—OK, not really. But I am from a family of eight card-toting siblings. Canasta's our game! While we play well together, family reunions can really be brutal! I mean, you can fall like a house of—well, you get the picture.

I've always wanted to learn to play Pinochle, so if that's your game, maybe you'd be willing to teach me.

I work as a nurse three days a week. It's a great job, not just because it feels good to help and nurture people, but it still gives me time to enjoy my life, too! On my days off, you'll find me at the yoga studio, swimming at the Y, visiting the new gallery at the Getty, or hiking up a Paramount mountain.

But, travel jolts my senses! My journeys have been life changing. So far, Ontario, Canada, is my favorite place to explore. It has European charm yet modern sophistication. Those Canadians are not just wonderfully warm people—they also sure do like to party. They are so fun to watch!

Now cooking is also something I like to watch, so if you are a barbecue king, I'll be there serving you a beer or a glass of wine!

My hope is that you are a guy who is happy, well-adjusted, and financially secure, with the time and energy to enjoy what life has to offer.

Oh—it helps if you're not allergic to my cat! She's a rescue, meaning she found me.

Maybe you will, too.

Proof

Made in the USA
Columbia, SC
15 February 2018